Conflicts of Interest:
Nonprofit Institutions

Conflicts of Interest:
Nonprofit Institutions

By Chris Welles

Report to the Twentieth Century Fund Steering Committee
on Conflicts of Interest in the Securities Markets

The Twentieth Century Fund/New York/1977

Library of Congress Catalog Card No. 77–78967
ISBN: 87078–142–1
Copyright © 1977 by The Twentieth Century Fund, Inc.
Manufactured in the United States of America

Foreword

Almost from its beginnings, the Twentieth Century Fund has had an interest in the functioning of the securities industry, which is so vital to the well-being of the American economy. One of its earliest research projects provided insight and information that influenced the legislation that created the Securities and Exchange Commission. Since then, the Fund has undertaken a number of projects in its continuing effort to help assure that the markets will perform honestly as well as efficiently. The present investigation of conflicts of interest in various sectors of the industry is the latest manifestation of this concern.

In order to deal effectively with the sensitive issue of conflicts, the Trustees of the Fund established a steering committee, headed by Roy A. Schotland, professor of law at Georgetown University Law School, to guide the work of its researcher analysts. The members of the steering committee are William L. Cary, Dwight Professor of Law at Columbia University School of Law and a former chairman of the SEC; Benjamin V. Cohen, a Trustee of the Fund who was the architect of much SEC legislation; Roger F. Murray, S. Sloan Colt Professor of Banking and Finance at Columbia University; and William Stott, former vice-president in charge of investments at Morgan Guaranty Trust Company. With Mr. Schotland and myself, the committee had many meetings in which policy recommendations were formulated and a series of investigations commissioned dealing with conflicts. The Fund is grateful to all the members of the committee for their time and effort.

Similarly, I want to express my appreciation for the work done by those who undertook the investigations of specific areas of conflict in the securities industry. They include John Brooks of the *New Yorker*, author of a number of books on Wall Street, including *The Go-Go Years;* Edward S. Herman, professor of finance at the Wharton School of the University of Pennsylvania and an eminent student of banking and finance; Louis M. Kohlmeier, a Pulitzer Prize winning journalist formerly with the *Wall Street Journal;* Martin Mayer, author of *The Bankers;* Nicholas Wolfson, a former staff member of the Securities and Exchange Commission who is now on the law faculty at the University of Connecticut; Richard Blodgett, editor of *The Corporate Communications Report* and author of the *New York Times Book of Money;* and Chris Welles, author of *The Last Days of the Club.* All had complete independence in writing their accounts. Their reports, first published separately in paperback form, will be included in a comprehensive book on conflicts that will also feature the policy recommendations of the steering committee.

M. J. Rossant, DIRECTOR
The Twentieth Century Fund
May 1977

Members of the Steering Committee

William L. Cary
Dwight Professor of Law
Columbia University

Benjamin V. Cohen
Lawyer, Washington, D. C.

Roger F. Murray
S. Sloan Colt Professor of
Banking and Finance
Columbia University

M. J. Rossant
Director
The Twentieth Century Fund

William Stott
William Stott Associates

Roy A. Schotland, Chairman
Professor of Law
Georgetown University

Contents

Preface
by Roy A. Schotland

Many forms of conduct permissible in a workaday world for those acting at arm's length are forbidden to those bound by fiduciary ties. A trustee is held to something stricter than the morals of the market place. Not honesty alone, but the punctilio of an honor the most sensitive, is then the standard of behavior. As to this there has developed a tradition that is unbending and inveterate. Uncompromising rigidity has been the attitude of courts of equity when petitioned to undermine the rule of undivided loyalty by the "disintegrating erosion" of particular exceptions. . . . Only thus has the level of conduct for fiduciaries been kept at a level higher than that trodden by the crowd.*

Almost half a century has passed since Benjamin Cardozo, then Chief Judge of New York, set forth this now classic description of the obligation of the fiduciary to act fairly in the interests of his clients. A year later came the stock market crash of 1929, which led to the Securities Act of 1933 and the Securities and Exchange Act of 1934, the most important and comprehensive securities market legislation in history.

Commenting on those events, in 1934 Justice Harlan Fiske Stone said:

I venture to assert that when the history of the financial era which has just drawn to a close comes to be written, most of its mistakes and its major faults will be ascribed to the failure to observe the fiduciary principle, the precept as old as Holy Writ, that "a man cannot serve two masters."**

---

* *Meinhard v. Salmon*, 249 N.Y. 458, 464, 164 N.E. 545, 546 (1928).

** "The Public Influence of the Bar," 48 *Harvard Law Review*, 1, 8.

Since those days the securities markets have operated reasonably efficiently and remained relatively free of scandal. Yet it is by no means clear that they have functioned as well as they might. In discussions at the Twentieth Century Fund in the early 1970s, a number of people with a great variety of involvements in the securities markets concluded that the "departure" of the small investor, perhaps some of the volatility of the market, and certainly much of the prevailing cynicism about Wall Street might be traced to a widespread, though generally not perceived, concern over conflicts of interest within the financial community. The Fund sponsored this study in an attempt to assess the pervasiveness of such conflicts of interest, to evaluate their significance, and to recommend realistic procedures for their resolution.

The overall study consists of a series of monographs, each focusing on the conflicts in one particular sector of the industry: commercial bank trust departments, broker-dealers, corporate pension funds, investment bankers, public (i.e., state and local pension funds, nonprofit institutions, and a complex investment medium—real estate investment trusts. The first five of these monographs will be released during 1975 and are summarized here.

The steering committee chose these institutions for several reasons. The first was their size. Bank trust departments, for example, manage about $400 billion of assets; private noninsured pension funds amount to approximately $125 billion. Second, those chosen operate primarily as fiduciaries and are therefore under a *legal* obligation to act in the interest of their customers. The conflict-of-interest abuses that arise in these environments quite properly arouse the greatest concern. Third, these institutions perform such a wide variety of functions that they are inescapably enmeshed in a maze of conflicting obligations which renders study of their problems and their resolution especially worthwhile. Although a lawyer in private practice faces conflicts of interest, they are neither as widespread nor remotely as complex as the conflicts faced by a firm that underwrites new issues, manages portfolios, markets investment advice, and executes transactions for both institutional and individual customers, as well as selling to them from its own inventory of securities. Finally, these institutions are sufficiently similar in structure and operations to permit comparisons of their respective approaches to conflict-of-interest problems.

Although the study was prepared under the general direction of a steering committee, each researcher worked independently and arrived at his own conclusions about the importance of the conflict-of-interest problem in the financial institution he examined.

The project's largest study, by Edward S. Herman, professor of finance at the University of Pennsylvania's Wharton School, is of commercial bank trust departments, which are part of an important industry with enormous—some would say excessive—economic power. How does the trust department vote proxies, especially if the stock is in a corporation which is a significant customer of the bank's commercial department? How does a bank regulate the flow of information it secures, in its capacity as creditor, about customers whose stock may be held in the trust department? How does a trust department allocate its information and attention among its hundreds or even thousands of accounts, some vastly larger and belonging to more "important" clients than others? These are among the difficult problems Herman examines.

Like trust departments, many broker-dealer firms must accommodate obligations to a large, varied group of investment management clients, handle both the invested cash and the securities of their customers fairly and efficiently, and prevent the use for investment purposes of any information that their principals may have if they serve on corporate boards. The report by Martin Mayer (author of *Wall Street: Men and Money* and *The Bankers*, among many other books) examines how broker-dealers deal with these problems. Mayer gives special attention to several unique conflicts of broker-dealers, such as the inherent tension between their advisory role and the brokerage compensation system, which has depended on the amount of trading, and the inherent conflict in the firm's roles as broker or agent in some transactions and as dealer or principal in others. The latter conflict becomes particularly complex in the familiar, much examined, and much regulated setting of the stock exchange specialist, as well as in the relatively new, immensely important, but little examined and little regulated setting of "block trading" firms.

In his paper Nicholas Wolfson, professor of law at the University of Connecticut School of Law, writes that underwriting raises unique—and perhaps uniquely acute—conflicts between obligations to the issuing corporation and to the public investors. More complex conflicts arise from the differences in the interests of the issuing corporation's stockholders, management, and the various classes of public investors. Wolfson follows these problems through the underwriting sequence, from selecting the underwriter and preparing the offering through pricing the issue, determining the underwriter's compensation, and providing an orderly trading market.

Pension funds are the largest category of investment portfolios; some are managed by trust departments, others by insurance companies, broker-dealers or investment advisors, or the sponsoring employer itself. The study of corporate pension funds is by John Brooks of the *New Yorker* magazine, author of *The Go-Go Years* and *Business Adventures*, among other books. State and local government pension funds are treated by Louis Kohlmeier, syndicated columnist and author of *Regulators: Watchdog Agencies and the Public Interest* and *God Save this Honorable Court: The Supreme Court Crisis*. Although Brooks and Kohlmeier consider some of the same questions that the other studies address, they also analyze such problems as the selection of investment management and the pressure to allocate brokerage commissions and custodian services to regional firms, which particularly characterize public pension funds. With the substantial increase in fiduciary protections provided by the Employee Retirement Income Security Act of 1974, which is just beginning to have an impact, it is timely to examine what problems pension funds have experienced and what new protections this legislation offers them. It is especially timely to consider such questions in the public fund setting, which is untouched by the new federal law.

Given the diversity of the backgrounds of the researchers and the independence enjoyed by each, it is not surprising that the studies vary widely in their approach. However, each author has endeavored to discover the major conflict situations, how and why they arise, what practices—both self-enforced and legally required—are followed to avoid abuse, and what if any evidence of abuse exists. Some authors have also considered whether corrective steps seem needed and what form they might take, a set of questions the steering committee will address at some length later when these monographs, now appearing separately, are published in a comprehensive book which will include an attempt to draw together the findings of each study and indicate what action and lines of further study seem appropriate.

The researchers and the members of the steering committee shared the problem of defining the term "conflict of interest." Conflict in the marketplace, or what the law calls "arm's-length" bargaining between buyer and seller, is not a conflict of interest in the sense of this project and related literature. Of course, all buyers and sellers are obligated not to be untruthful, and in some situations sellers may have special duties, for example, when a buyer relies upon a seller to select an article for a particular use. But we do not think of such obligations as fiduciary nor of such situations as conflicts of interest, and despite the similarities between such situations and fiduciary ones, the differences lead to important distinctions. For all the difficulty purchasers may have in selecting a bottle of wine or repairing a television set, the commercial marketplace generally does an efficient and effective job of resolving the conflict between buyer and seller; at worst, the buyers lose a few dollars and switch to another seller.

In the marketplace for professional services, such as medical treatment, legal advice, and investment management, the situation is different. First, the need or wish for confidentiality makes marketplace-type shopping unfeasible. Second, the importance of the service rendered makes the cost of a mistake too high to justify reliance on the trial and error approach that a consumer may use in the commercial marketplace. Finally, the buyer is simply unable to evaluate not only the worth of the services but even what services are required. Even after the transaction has been completed, it is hard for the buyer to determine whether the service was appropriate and the fee reasonable. The combination of these conditions has led the law to invite buyers of professional services to put aside caveat emptor and to repose trust in the seller.

In the securities field, this trust is expressed in the fiduciary obligations of the brokers, dealers, lawyers, accountants, pension fund officials, bankers, underwriters, and other professionals who intermediate between buyers and sellers of securities. Of course, legislating a principle does not guarantee a result; there are unprofessional professionals and faithless fiduciaries. But it does reflect and support the expectation of special conduct and impose the burden of unique responsibilities.

Indeed, it is imperative to recognize that the self-serving opportunities present in conflict-of-interest situations are usually not exploited. If such were not the case, fiduciary relationships would seldom have survived, reputations would rarely be intact, and the law would have had to intervene far more frequently than it has. Throughout these studies, conflicts in which improper favoritism or self-serving *could* occur have been kept distinct from those conflicts in which actual abuses *have* occurred.

Our main concern has been to explore the occurrence of actual abuses and the adequacy of safeguards against future abuse. Actual abuses, even if infrequent, are important because they inflict injuries and arouse fears. When someone in a position of trust takes an improper economic advantage, he or she deprives some individuals of what is rightfully theirs and hurts others by lowering the operating efficiency of firms, causing inefficient allocation of resources, or both. Such injuries occur with sufficient frequency and seriousness to justify business and government in taking corrective measures, although these measures are not without their own costs.

Examination of the necessity and appropriateness of these measures is important. In these areas, the researchers found ample cause for concern. For example, as Herman recounts, for decades the major banks used a large part of their trust account brokerage commissions to attract demand deposits that benefited the shareholders of the bank rather than the trust accounts that should rightfully have benefited from those funds. Although antitrust suits and changes in brokerage commission structure have largely solved that problem, other problems, such as the placement of trust accounts' uninvested cash in non-interest-bearing deposits in the trust department's own bank, remain acute. Or as Wolfson points out in his description of one underwriting, it is far too easy for the investment banker who also serves as an investment manager to exploit this dual role to the disadvantage of the public.

Conflicts of interest also matter because of appearances. As Kohlmeier demonstrates in his study of state and municipal pension funds, when a banker sits on the board of a public pension fund but also manages that fund's equity investments, holds its cash deposits, and makes its mortgage investments, it is hard to persuade outsiders that the fund is being administered in the best interests of its beneficiaries, no matter how selflessly the banker may be fulfilling his responsibilities. Or as Brooks suggests in his study, even if a corporate pension fund that purchases the stock of the sponsoring corporation sincerely believes that those securities are a wise investment, the conflict of interest is so obvious that many corporations strictly prohibit this practice, and federal law now limits it. To the extent that major firms in the securities industry fail to provide the appearance as well as the reality of abuse-free behavior, the entire industry becomes suspect and legal intervention becomes more likely.

It is easy to urge that all conflict-of-interest situations be eliminated, until one considers the cost of "purifying" the system. Some would argue, for example, that broker-dealers should not be permitted to be underwriters as well. Yet as Wolfson points out in his study of investment bankers, segregating underwriters would surely be an extremely costly solution and, worse, would probably not even achieve the benefits that its advocates claim. As Mayer puts the problem in his study: "Many conflicts are unavoidable: like thermal pollution from a power plant, they are the externalities of productive behavior. The question is whether institutional arrangements enlarge or diminish the uninvited harm done by such conflicts, and whether the costs of changing the arrangements exceed the benefits derived."

Consequently, some who read these papers may well be disappointed that more radical changes have not been recommended. At the same time, others may be disappointed that the securities profession is not viewed as favorably as they perhaps would like. The papers may, indeed, invite comment, even controversy. In the faith that such a response will enhance the illumination and resolution of these problems, all those involved in this project welcome reactions from interested persons, confident that discussion will enrich the final product, a comprehensive book including all the papers as well as the steering committee's summary of their findings and what policy changes these findings suggest.

As Justice Felix Frankfurter wrote some thirty years ago: "To say that a man is a fiduciary only begins analysis."* The Twentieth Century Fund study of conflicts of interest in the securities markets is dedicated to the continuing analysis of fiduciary responsibilities.

---

*SEC v. Chenery Corp., 318 U.S. 80, 85-6 (1943).

Nonprofit Institutions

For valuable assistance in assembling research material for this report, I would like to thank Randy Gilbert of the Twentieth Century Fund staff.

Author's Preface

As a journalist, I approached the task of reporting on conflicts of interest in nonprofit institutions somewhat differently than an academic researcher. Although I read and studied reports from over two hundred endowment funds and foundations, as well as much other material, the findings of fact and conclusions of this report are not based on rigorous statistical analyses or formal surveys and questionnaires. My research consisted primarily of wide-ranging interviews with various individuals who I felt might be knowledgeable about what conflicts of interest exist, how serious they are, and what ought to be done about them. Having weighed and judged the diverse viewpoints I encountered and having examined as much information as I could obtain from endowment funds and foundations, I gradually developed my own conclusions.

This report focuses principally on foundations and educational endowments. Although such institutions as hospitals, symphony orchestras, ballet companies, and museums also operate on a nonprofit basis, foundations and educational endowments hold the bulk of the assets in this category.* (Churches also hold immense assets, but because they are subject to few disclosure requirements, little information is available to the public about their holdings or financial operations.) According to figures compiled by the New York Stock Exchange (NYSE), as of 1975, foundations owned $22.1 billion in NYSE-listed stocks, educational endowments owned $7.2 billion, and all other nonprofit organizations owned $8.7 billion.[1] In 1975, the Securities and Exchange Commission, which does not compile data on nonprofit institutions other than foundations and endowments, put the total assets of foundations at $34.2 bil-

---

*There are a few significant exceptions. For example, when he died in June 1976, J. Paul Getty left his 21.5 percent interest in the Getty Oil Co., now worth $750 million, to the J. Paul Getty Museum in Malibu, California. As a result, the endowment of this museum is probably larger than that of all the country's other museums put together.

lion and those of educational endowments at $13.8 billion.[2] If the other nonprofit institutions invested a similar portion of their assets in NYSE stocks, the total assets of nonprofit institutions would amount to about $62 billion (slightly less than the $66 billion held by mutual funds[3]), of which foundations and endowments would account for about 77 percent.

The investment-related conflicts of interest to which foundations and educational endowments are prone seem quite similar to those of other nonprofit institutions. The basic problem is that all nonprofit institutions, particularly those that receive contributions from affluent donors or investment income from endowments, depend on benefactors from the business world. Thousands of nonprofit institutions are unable to obtain sufficient support from government programs, operating income, or donations from the general public. Businessmen and those associated with business wealth enable these institutions to survive. Businessmen and their heirs are virtually the only creators of private foundations, which themselves are important sources of funding for other nonprofit institutions. Although these individuals are generally well intentioned, they sometimes have difficulty separating their philanthropic and fiduciary activities from their personal business interests. When they permit the latter to take precedence over the former, the conflict of interest inherent in their situation degenerates into abuse, and the affected nonprofit institution, as well as its beneficiaries, inevitably suffers.

My research suggests that although conflicts of interest and conflict abuses in foundations and educational endowments may be less serious now than in the past, they still remain widespread. Surprisingly little action is being taken to combat them. In response to some particularly lurid revelations in the 1960s, the Tax Reform Act of 1969 imposed some important controls on private foundations. Yet several major problem areas were relatively unaffected by the act and continue to breed abuses. No federal laws and only a few, generally very mild or unenforced, state laws deal with conflicts of interest in other nonprofit institutions. But recent events indicate that unless trustees of nonprofit institutions take the initiative in purging their organizations of conflict-of-interest problems, they will eventually face a new wave of public criticism, legal challenges, and perhaps even new federal legislation.

Educational
Endowments

I/Introduction

In 1966, Ford Foundation president McGeorge Bundy made his now fa-
mous observation that "over the long run caution has cost our colleges
and universities much more than imprudence or risk-taking."[1] This criticism, reinforced in later pronouncements by the Ford Foundation,[2]
spurred a massive overhaul of investment policies at many colleges and
universities. A large number of schools, which had invested heavily in
fixed-income securities and steadfastly eschewed all but minor commitments in equities, hastily built up their stock portfolios. They made their
purchases at what proved to be the peak of the 1960s bull market.[3] During the inflationary-recessionary 1970s, of course, many endowment
managers wished they had held onto their pre-Bundy portfolios.

But Bundy's statement also led to beneficial change in the way many
colleges and universities managed their endowment funds. Previously,
according to Roger F. Murray, professor of banking and finance at Columbia University and a man with wide experience in nonprofit institutions, many if not most funds utilized "management by crony."* The
funds were often little more than the private preserves of the schools'
boards of trustees; often, they were incestuous hotbeds of interest conflicts and abuses. In many cases, the funds' investment advisors, banks,

*When no source is given for a quotation, it may be assumed that the state-
ments were derived from interviews with the author between November 1976
and January 1977. When the quoted individual is not identified by name or institution, it is because the person would talk with the author only if his or her name
was withheld, usually because of the sensitivity of the matter being discussed.

7

and brokers were so tightly involved with the schools' trustees, donors, and alumni that the interests of the fund and the school were lost in a tangle of cozy self-dealing and mutual back-scratching. Not only the public but even such concerned beneficiaries of the funds as students and faculty members were usually ignorant of these relationships because most funds released little if any substantive information about investment policies, portfolio composition, or the identities of their managers or advisors. In a 1970 article in the Philadelphia *Evening Bulletin*, business writer J. A. Livingston has provided an illuminating example of the sort of conflict situation common during this period.[4]

For many years prior to the bankruptcy of Penn Central in 1970, Howard Butcher III, a senior partner of Butcher & Sherrerd, one of Philadelphia's largest brokerage houses, had been a trustee and chairman of the investment committee at the University of Pennsylvania. Butcher was not only a Penn alumnus but also one of Penn's most important donors. At the same time, his firm was the paid investment advisor to and one of the principal brokers for the university's $100 million endowment fund. Butcher also was on the board of the Penn Central Railroad Company. At one time, he had been the largest individual holder of Penn Central stock, and he had been instrumental in bringing about the merger between the Pennsylvania Railroad and the New York Central. Butcher was an enthusiastic booster of Penn Central's stock; at his urging, his family, several friends, and a number of his firm's customers had become major stockholders. His firm also was a holder and an underwriter of Penn Central securities issues. At Butcher's recommendation, the University of Pennsylvania's endowment fund had paid more than $8 million for 113,214 shares. This block was the largest in the university's portfolio, except for American Telephone & Telegraph Co. The university's president, Gaylord P. Harnwell, was on the railroad's board as well.

During 1969 and 1970, Penn Central's fortunes began faltering badly. Butcher, convinced the troubles were only temporary, steadfastly refused to lighten the university's holdings. For a time, he even disregarded the instructions of the rest of the investment committee to unload. Only when Penn Central's difficulties became so extreme that even Butcher could no longer overlook them did he commence a wholesale dumping of the stock. Yet according to Livingston, Butcher was more diligent in disposing of his, his family's, and his friend's Penn Central holdings than of the university's. The price of the railroad's stock was falling steadily, and because, on average, the university's shares were sold later than those of the other holders whom Butcher advised, Penn realized a lower average price per share than the other holders. According to Livingston, this delay may have cost the university as much as $279,639; the university's total loss on its Penn Central investment was $3,029,807.

Butcher himself does not dispute Livingston's figures, but he denies any deliberate wrongdoing. In putting Penn into the stock, he maintains, "I thought I was doing the best thing for the university. It was just bad judgment on my part." But if Howard Butcher and his firm had not been so tightly involved with Penn Central, the university might have acquired fewer Penn Central shares, sold them sooner, and lost less money.

Bundy's recommendations have helped endowments in a number of cases to free themselves from incestuous relationships of this type. In recent years, trustees at many schools have retained independent investment managers, whose selection has been based solely on competence and cost, in order to improve investment performance and reduce the potential for conflict-of-interest abuses. While retaining the right to establish broad guidelines, the boards of many endowments have given the managers complete discretion in making specific portfolio selections. A few schools with large endowments, such as Harvard and the University of California, have established professional in-house management teams who also enjoy considerable discretion to assemble portfolios under broad guidelines laid down by the trustees. Increasingly, trustees designate custodian banks and brokers solely on the basis of competence, performance, and cost.[5] Many schools now publish detailed financial reports containing descriptions of investment policy, breakdowns of portfolio holdings, and reports on investment performance.

As a result of these developments, when I began my research for this report, I assumed that the traditional management by crony form of conflict of interest had all but disappeared and that the principal problem area now lay in the rapidly expanding partnerships among educational institutions, corporations, and the government.[6] Colleges and universities today are major recipients of corporate and government grants and are frequent partners with corporations in research ventures. For example, in North Carolina, Duke University, the University of North Carolina, and North Carolina State University have joined forces to build and maintain a 5,200-acre enterprise known as Research Triangle Park. The park houses government and industrial tenants including the U.S. Army, the Environmental Protection Agency, IBM, Monsanto, Becton Dickinson, and Richardson-Merrell. Among other things, the three schools share the surpluses of the nonprofit foundation that operates the park and maintain a joint research institute that provides services to industrial and government tenants. According to a Research Triangle Park brochure:

> The faculties and technically skilled staffs of the three schools work closely with Triangle industrial and government personnel in a wide variety of fields involving planning and execution of cooperative research. Such association has resulted in close personal relationships and the free exchange of information of mutual interest.

Other colleges are going into business themselves, establishing subsidiary corporations to purchase revenue-producing property. Jerome P. Keuper, president of the Florida Institute of Technology, which operates several for-profit subsidiaries, has been quoted as saying, "We're going to get into anything that looks profitable, is honest, and doesn't compete unfairly with business in our community."[7]

These trends may, over time, lead universities to orient their curricula, or the thrust and philosophy of their educational services, toward furthering their outside relationships rather than toward meeting the needs of their students. This shift may already be taking place. One observer sees

> . . . a coalescence of higher education and business that is a radical departure from the older notion of the university as an independent seeker of truth, beholden to no one.

> In the past the university was relied upon to serve as a social critic, insulated from the kinds of pressures that inevitably dictate accommodation in business and government. Today that independence is rapidly being lost as the universities join with industry and government in mutually appealing endeavors.[8]

Universities, of course, have never been as independent or as insulated as this quotation suggests. Yet whatever the broader implications and problems presented by this coalescence, no informed observer questioned for this report considered its impact on the investment of educational endowment funds to be significant. Of course, the alliance of universities, industry, and government may yet generate conflicts of interest and actual abuses at educational endowment funds, but at present, the main conflict-of-interest problem of endowments is still management by crony.

Although many institutions have made significant progress in this area, the improvement over the pre-Bundy days amounts to less than is generally believed. Conflicts as blatant as those in the Penn Central episode at the University of Pennsylvania are unusual, and instances of deliberate self-enrichment by fiduciaries appear to be very rare. But boards of trustees that rigorously maintain arm's-length relationships and pursue the best interests of the endowment fund above all still tend to be more the exception than the rule. And in far too many cases, colleges and universities still consider management of their endowment funds to be a private matter between the school and its trustees and refuse to release anything more than the most rudimentary data about their funds.*

The available information suggests the prevalence of a number of conflict-of-interest problems:

• A businessman who is a trustee of a university gives the school a large block of his company's stock. Although the endowment fund's managers are technically free to dispose of the block if they judge it to be unsuitable for their portfolio, they hold it for fear of antagonizing or upsetting the donor, who clearly believes that his company's stock is a good investment. As a result, the school's portfolio is insufficiently diversified and thus excessively risky. If gifts to the fund are pooled and the fund, because of the large block it is holding, performs badly or has a very low yield, the contributions of other donors also diminish in value. Moreover, in such situations as tender offers, management compensation plans, and shareholder resolutions, the trustees and managers invariably vote the block in favor of management, even though doing so may not be in the best interests of the institution as a stockholder.

• Some endowment funds deal with investment advisors whose officers serve on the boards of trustees or who are associated with major donors and fund-raisers, rather than seek out the best and least expensive advisory services regardless of such associations. Other funds are internally managed, and the trustees' investment committees are heavily involved in stock selection. When the portfolio does not perform well, the other trustees are reluctant to be as critical of their peers, friends, and business associates or as eager to alter investment procedures as they would be if the portfolio were being managed by an outsider.

---

*For this study, financial reports were obtained from ninety-three universities, colleges, and private schools. Only twenty-eight contained breakdowns of portfolio composition. After follow-up requests, several other institutions supplied portfolio data. But some did so only on the condition that the data not be released. Others refused to supply any further data.

• When trustees are involved in the stock selection process or the advisor is linked to the trustees, the fund tends to invest in companies with ties to the trustees. This favoritism is not based on some nefarious scheme to manipulate stock prices but is a natural by-product of mutual friendship, nourishment, and support. But the portfolio that results is seldom what a disinterested manager would have chosen and may not be in the best interests of the fund.

• Instead of making use of firms that offer the best executions at the lowest price, a fund directs brokerage commissions to firms associated with the school's important donors, fund-raisers, and trustees. Similarly, the fund maintains banking and custodial relationships with institutions selected not for the high quality and low cost of their services but for their ties to trustees, donors, and fund-raisers.

To the extent that considerations other than the interests of the endowment fund influence the selection of its managers, advisors, and banks, they inhibit efforts to obtain services at the lowest cost and to achieve the best performance. Hence, they may impose on colleges and universities costs that are unnecessary and totally unjustifiable, given the financial plights of many schools. But such costs are difficult to measure, and they may not be large. According to one estimate, a typical endowment fund's custodial, administrative, professional, and brokerage costs per year are about 0.5 percent of average assets.[9] Fees to an outside manager may run between 0.1 percent and 1 percent. Paying at a rate of 1 percent of assets for all these expenses, a $50 million fund would incur total costs of $500,000 annually. Of course, a portfolio containing a large block of donor stock may not necessarily perform worse than a more disinterestedly assembled portfolio, and a trustee-linked investment manager may not necessarily achieve less satisfactory results than a disinterestedly selected manager. Moreover, the contribution of endowment fund income to college and university budgets is low and continues to decline. A survey of 214 colleges and universities indicates that, as of 1971, endowment income accounted for only 6.9 percent of the schools' total income.[10] Although endowment income is more important to independent institutions, whose financial health is sometimes precarious, than to state-supported institutions, the direct financial cost of endowment fund conflict-of-interest abuses is probably small relative to the other expenses of the average college or university.

Other costs, although less quantifiable, may be more significant. Since Watergate, public concern has focused on the ethical conduct of the nation's institutions. In the past, the trustees of nonprofit institutions tended to regard themselves as free of the outside scrutiny and accountability to which corporate board members were properly subject. Even today, very few colleges or universities have adopted a formal conflict-of-interest policy for their endowment funds. According to one observer:

> Since there are no "owners" in the ordinary sense of the term, no specific beneficiaries, no general or uniform rules for the disclosure of financial or other types of information, nonprofit trustees in effect are not answerable to anyone. Within very broad limits, they are their own masters. The words "irresponsible power" are harsh words, but they are relevant. . . . The trustee's problem is compounded—or simplified, depending on the point of view—by the absence of any systematic, generally accepted criteria that define satisfactory performance on their part.[11]

As a result of some recent events, though, trustees are now in danger of losing some of this freedom. In compliance with recently adopted accounting standards, colleges and universities, as well as other nonprofit institutions, may soon be including in their financial statements lists of "related party transactions," many of which may carry conflict-of-interest potential. Such disclosure should focus public attention on once secret relationships, such as links between trustees and investment managers. Moreover, a recent court finding[12] that the trustees of a nonprofit hospital had breached their fiduciary duty through self-dealing and other abuses may have set a precedent, according to some attorneys, for similar court actions against college and university trustees.

Lawsuits are not the only potential problem. To a much greater degree, perhaps, than any other single group of institutions (with the possible exception of churches), colleges and universities are viewed by the public as examples of ethical conduct. Schools that permit questionable practices in the management of their endowments may increasingly find themselves subjected to embarrassing and damaging criticism.

To be sure, trustees and university officials have made substantial progress in bringing impartial, professional management to endowment funds. Yet the evidence indicates that there is still a long way to go before the regrettable traditions of management by crony are completely expunged.

II/The Trustees

The root of most endowment fund conflicts of interest is the trustee. Formally, the board of trustees of a nonprofit institution, like the board of directors of a for-profit corporation, is the principal policymaking body. In addition, nonprofit institutions, much more than corporations, use board membership as an honorific mechanism; at colleges and universities, board membership serves to fortify the school's ties with its major benefactors and fund-raisers, whose philanthropic contributions are often critical to the school's financial health. Since most wealth is business wealth, many trustees, as well as other important donors and fund-raisers, are businessmen, usually chairmen and presidents of corporations located in the same geographical area as the school. Richard Aldrich of the Association of Governing Boards, which collects data on the subject, estimates that 5,000 corporate executives may be serving as college and university trustees. The concern that businessmen feel for the success of a local college or university is not always purely altruistic. The presence of a nearby, highly regarded school lends prestige to their own businesses. The school also may be useful as a source of research and development assistance and new recruits, a purchaser of corporate products and services, or simply a general boon to the regional economy.

Many colleges and universities are inextricable components of their respective communities' industrial and financial power structures. A researcher seeking to identify the business establishment of a city might find the listing of trustees of a local college or university a good place to start. For example, the seventy-member board of trustees of Case Western Reserve University in Cleveland includes present or former executives of five of the seven largest industrial corporations headquartered in Cleveland—TRW, Inc., Republic Steel Corp., the B. F. Goodrich Co., Standard Oil Company (Ohio), and Eaton Corp.— as well as executives from the city's two largest banks, Cleveland Trust Co. and National City Bank of Cleveland. About three-quarters of the trustees have business affiliations. Among the numerous close links between Case Western Reserve and local business interests is University Circle Research Center, a $100 million industrial research project established by the university and local businesses.

Similarly, Northeastern University in Boston includes among its 175 corporation officers senior executives from such Boston-area concerns as Raytheon Co., New England Telephone & Telegraph Co., Foxboro Co., USM Corp., Foster Grant Co., Boston Edison Co., Arthur D. Little, Inc., the Gillette Co., Sprague Electric Co., and Polaroid Corp. It also includes representatives of Boston's financial community: The Boston Co., State Street Bank and Trust Co., First National Bank of Boston, New England Merchants National Bank, National Shawmut Bank of Boston, New England Mutual Life Insurance Co., John Hancock Mutual Life Insurance Co., Liberty Mutual Insurance Co., Massachusetts Financial Services, Inc., and Putnam Management Co. Over three-quarters of the officers of the Northeastern Corp. are businessmen.

Despite the formal extent of their authority over the institutions on whose boards they sit, college and university trustees, like the trustees of other nonprofit institutions, usually lack the time or the inclination to become very deeply involved in the schools' affairs. Perhaps as a result, as one observer has put it:

[M]ost trustees simply do not understand the "nitty gritty," "day-to-day," "real world" work of the hospital, museum, dance company, university, or foundation that has invited them to serve. (And they would be the first to say so. The invitation to serve is a civic honor that is hard to turn down.) Trustees, well intentioned as they usually are, often are quite unfamiliar with the operations, budgeting, and spending of the institution. So these "operating finances" or expenditures are usually left entirely to the administration. On the other hand, the responsibility for income is divided into three parts. The administration is responsible for setting fees for admission, membership, tuition, and so forth. The administration divides with trustees the responsibility for fund raising. And the trustees, usually without a clear knowledge of the current financial future of the institutions they are striving to serve, are given full responsibility for the endowment. (After all, they're financial people. And besides, what else can they do?)[1]

The legal obligations of trustees in managing college and university endowment funds have never been clearly spelled out: "There is virtually no statutory law regarding trustees or governing boards of eleemosynary institutions, and case law is sparse."[2] A recent judicial decision regarding trust funds states that trustees have a duty to "maximize the trust income by prudent investment."[3] Directors and trustees of nonprofit institutions also are considered "obligated to act in the utmost good faith and to exercise ordinary business care and prudence in all matters affecting the management" of the organization.[4] Good faith, prudence, and care would seem to require that trustees maintain a "Chinese wall" between the investment of the endowment fund's assets and their own personal financial interests.

Many trustees strive diligently and successfully to maintain that Chinese wall. Francis Fenn, executive director of the National Association of College and University Business Officers, contends that "trustees often rise above themselves when they take on the responsibility [of being trustees] and become much more statesmanlike and ethical than before." Hazel Sanger of Thorndike, Doran, Paine & Lewis in Atlanta, which acts as investment manager for several endowment funds, says, "We see a very general shift in the direction of avoiding any appearance of conflicts of interest.* Trustees are becoming increasingly scrupulous."

Yet at fund after fund, portfolio investments and the suppliers of financial services to the fund are linked to the outside business and financial affiliations of the trustees and of important donors and fundraisers. The management of the trust fund is not isolated from the tight interrelationships among the school, its trustees, and local businesses, but is a part of those interrelationships.

It is important to understand the atmosphere and context in which the overwhelming majority of these conflicts and abuses occur. The trustees involved are not dishonest individuals furtively conspiring to channel business to friends or to enrich themselves at the fund's expense. Rather, they are essentially well-meaning, basically honorable individuals en-

---

*Like Hazel Sanger, many people use the term "conflict of interest" to signify an actual abuse. In this paper, that term refers to a situation in which an individual has two opposing interests, usually his obligations as a fiduciary and trustee and his private financial interests. Such a situation is not inherently improper. But a conflict of interest may lead to abuse when the individual does not keep his conflicting interests separate, when, for instance, he permits his private interests to interfere with his performance as a fiduciary, to the detriment of the institution involved.

gaging in practices with which they sincerely see nothing wrong. In many cases, trustees feel that a little business from the fund for their corporation is a justifiable quid pro quo for the time they contribute to the institution by serving on the board.

Despite their nonprofit status, colleges and universities experience many of the same financial problems as profit-making corporations. But perhaps because they need not show a profit, trustees still tend to regard them as institutions to which accepted practices of good business are not applicable. "The things that govern your behavior in your own business do not seem to apply when you become a trustee," says Hans H. Jenny, vice-president for finance and business at the College of Wooster in Ohio. "You're making the same kinds of decisions. But your behavior changes, and you tolerate things you wouldn't sit still for in your own business." For example, in overseeing the management of a corporation's pension fund, the performance of which directly affects the corporation's earnings, a corporate executive typically conducts an elaborate competition to secure the best managers and does not hesitate to fire a manager who performs poorly. He will assiduously demand that whoever manages the fund shop diligently for brokerage and custodial services. He will make sure that the portfolio includes nothing but those securities most likely to produce the greatest return at the designated risk level. Yet in his capacity as a college or university trustee, the same individual often sees nothing wrong in allocating fund commission business to firms associated with a well-known alumnus, selecting as investment manager a firm run by an important donor, and permitting the portfolio to hold securities chosen not for their investment merits but because they are associated with other trustees.

It is from this still prevalent double standard that the worst conflict-of-interest abuses at endowment funds flow.

III/The Portfolio

The most visible evidence of the breach in the Chinese wall between the interests of endowment funds and the private interests of trustees, as well as donors and fund-raisers, is the presence in endowment fund portfolios of securities linked to the business affiliations of the trustees.* Most often, positions in these securities are the result of gifts from trustees that the managers of the fund have chosen to hold. Gifts of appreciated securities are popular, of course, because the donor can deduct the full market value of the gift when he makes it and need not pay a capital gains tax on long-term holdings. In some cases, the trustees themselves have supervised purchases by the fund of stock in their own companies. Some examples of apparent trustee influence on portfolios:

- As of August 31, 1976, Emory University's endowments and trust funds had a market value of $169,708,000. Some 46.5 percent of that, or $78,737,000, was invested in a single company: the Coca-Cola Co. Emory has long been closely linked to large individual holders of Coca-Cola stock, particularly members of the Woodruff and Candler families, whose gifts of stock account for most of Emory's holdings.

*Unless otherwise indicated, data on endowment holdings and trustee identifications were derived from the college or university's latest published financial report, supplemented, in cases where they were not part of the financial report, by schedules of portfolio investments supplied at the request of the author. Additional information about investment policies was obtained from interviews with treasurers and other individuals associated with or knowledgeable about the funds.

Charles W. Duncan, Jr., former president of Coca-Cola, was a member of the boards of both Coca-Cola and Emory until his recent appointment as Deputy Secretary of Defense. Emory's vice-president for health affairs is on Coca-Cola's board. George Woodruff and C. Howard Candler, from whose family the Woodruffs purchased Coca-Cola in 1919, are listed as trustees emeriti. Emory has a total of thirty-three trustees on its board.

• Close to 40 percent of the University of Rochester's $342,523,655 worth of endowment assets, as of December 31, 1975, consisted of two stocks: 825,000 shares of Eastman Kodak Co., worth $87,553,000, and 735,000 shares of Xerox Corp., worth $37,393,000. Executives of the two companies have been major benefactors of the university. Three executives of Kodak, including the chairman and the president, and two executives of Xerox, including the chairman, sit on the university's thirty-four-member board of trustees. The endowment fund also holds positions in Sybron Corp., Lincoln First Banks, Inc., and Security New York State Corp. All these concerns have their headquarters in Rochester, and their chief executives (or, in the case of Lincoln First Banks, that of the local bank of which Lincoln First Banks is the holding company) are trustees of the university. W. Allen Wallis, chancellor of the university, is a director of Eastman Kodak and Lincoln First Banks. Emanuel Goldberg, a board member of Sybron, is head of the university trustees' investment committee. The endowment fund's positions in Kodak, Xerox, Lincoln First Banks, Security New York, and Sybron were acquired in part through purchases on the open market.

• The largest single equity position in the $63,063,078 portfolio of endowment and similar funds held by Swarthmore College, as of June 30, 1976, was 68,976 shares of Standard Pressed Steel Co., worth $1,043,662. Most or all of this stock was a gift from H. Thomas Hallowell, Jr., chairman of Standard Pressed Steel. Hallowell is a member of Swarthmore's thirty-four-member board of trustees and its investment committee. Swarthmore also owns 56,344 shares of Scott Paper Co. worth $855,090, largely acquired through gifts from Thomas B. McCabe, a former chairman of Scott Paper who, for many years, was chairman of Swarthmore's investment committee. The current finance committee chairman at Swarthmore is J. Lawrence Shane, Scott Paper's chief financial officer.

• As of June 30, 1976, Washington University in St. Louis held $158,173,000 in endowment and similar funds. Included in its portfolio, as of November 30, 1976, were positions in Interco, Inc., The May Department Stores Co., McDonnell Douglas Corp., Mercantile Bancorporation, Inc., Mallinckrodt, Inc., Monsanto Co., and Olin Corp. Included on its forty-nine-member board of trustees were executives or directors of those concerns, all of which are located in St. Louis. Families linked to several of the companies, such as Olin, Mallinckrodt, and McDonnell Douglas, have made sizable gifts to the university. The co-chairmen of Washington University's investment committee are the chairman of Interco and the honorary chairman of Olin. The fund acquired several of its trustee-linked investments, including Monsanto and Interco, largely on the open market.

• Northwestern University's $225,667,868 portfolio of endowment and similar funds, as of July 31, 1976, held positions in American Hospital Supply Corp., Combined Communications Corp., Continental Illinois Corp., Illinois Tool Works, Inc., Johnson Products Co., First Chicago Corp., G. D. Searle & Co., Sears Roebuck & Co., and Standard Oil Co. of Indiana. Executives of these companies, which have their headquarters in the Chicago area, are on Northwestern's thirty-eight-member board of trustees. The university acquired its two largest blocks of stock, $17,378,932 worth of American Hospital Supply and $8,952,510 worth of Searle, as gifts. Daniel C. Searle, chief executive of G. D. Searle, and Karl D. Bays, chief executive of American Hospital Supply, are trustees of the university. The head of Northwestern's investment committee is John J. Louis, Jr., chairman of Combined Communications; Northwestern holds 50,550 shares of his company's stock, acquired on the open market and valued at $524,456.The university acquired at least part of its holdings of other trustee-linked securities—including Illinois Tool Works, Johnson Products, Standard Oil of Indiana, and Continental Illinois—on the open market. Harold B. Smith, president of Illinois Tool; Blaine J. Yarrington, executive vice-president of Standard Oil of Indiana; and Tilden Cummings, formerly president and still a director of Continental Illinois, are on the investment committee with John Louis.

These colleges and universities publish lists of their portfolio investments. Many others do not. One such institution is the California Institute of Technology, which, as of June 30, 1976, had $145,241,000 in endowment and similar funds. Henry J. Tanner, Caltech's assistant treasurer, reports that it is a policy of the trustees not to release investment data. "I don't know if it is really something we want the public to know," he states. "Why should we?" Tanner goes on to explain:

> We have quite a broad board of trustees, and some of the stock in their companies is held out of proportion to what might be held in the average portfolio. We have some holdings of a substantial size in certain companies that are not normally held. This may be one sensitive reason. Mr. X may have given us some shares in his company and he might not like the outside world to realize he had done this.

Caltech's forty-member board includes the presidents or chairmen of such major West Coast corporations as Atlantic Richfield Co., Rockwell International Corp., Union Oil Co. of California, TRW, Inc., Twentieth Century-Fox Film Corp., MCA, Inc., Security Pacific Corp., Bank-America Corp., Wells Fargo & Co., and Pacific Mutual Life Insurance Co. Most of these executives or their companies are important donors to Caltech and sponsors of various university programs. Twenty-two corporation executives who are trustees are members of "visiting committees" who "play a vital role in directing the future development of education and research at the California Institute of Technology."[1]

Of course, not all trustee-linked investments are harmful to the interests of the universities involved. The University of Rochester has unquestionably benefited from its Kodak and Xerox holdings. But most such acquisitions are less successful. In 1969, at the urging of a trustee, Worcester Polytechnic Institute, which has an endowment of $27.3 million, put $6 million in a private placement mutual fund that had just been organized by the Paul Revere Life Insurance Co. The trustee was an officer of the mutual fund. "It went nowhere but downhill and didn't even pay us a dividend," recalls WPI treasurer David E. Lloyd. Finally, after the school had suffered a loss of about $1.5 million, the trustee recommended that the stock be sold and WPI unloaded its position. "It really killed us," says Lloyd. "We don't even like to think about it."

This investment involved a conspicuous risk. But even some relatively more conservative trustee-linked investments seem inappropriate for a university endowment. For example, in the past four years, the price of Combined Communications Corp. stock has declined by 50 percent, and the company is forbidden by loan agreements to pay a dividend. The stock's price volatility has been 50 percent greater than the New York Stock Exchange average. The market value of Northwestern's position in this stock, according to the university's latest report, was about $1 million less than its book value. Similarly, Coca-Cola stock is selling at half its price of three years ago, and it has recently been yielding about 3 percent.

Publicly, most treasurers assert that their endowments maintain positions in trustee-linked securities strictly for their investment merits. "They represent our best investment judgment," says John B. Borsch, Jr., director of the investment department at Northwestern, which manages its fund internally. "I have never really felt any inhibition in regard to our securities holdings simply because there was a trustee involved."

A few university officials publicly admit to the presence of other considerations. "If the stock is considered investment grade," says Merl M. Huntsinger, treasurer of Washington University, "we have a policy, if we get a big gift of stock and we know there is more stock out there, of hanging on to it." But most university officials, as well as outside investment managers and trustees, will only discuss such considerations anonymously.

"There are plenty of cases where universities feel a reluctance to dump the stock," says the head of an investment advisory firm with a number of endowment clients. "They feel that if they don't antagonize the donor, he'll give them more stock."

"There are circumstances under which this college continues to hold a certain stock because of the personal relationship involved," says the treasurer of one southern college. "We will not offend a significant donor to the college or an important trustee by apparently expressing some doubts about his company. Take our big holding of ——— [a company in which his fund held a large block]. It may not be a very good investment. But on the other hand, it didn't cost us anything." Asked why an eastern university continues to hold a large block of stock donated by one of its trustees, the trustee in question responds, "Nothing has ever been said about that, either by them [the college's investment officers] or by me. But there is a kind of understanding about . . . well . . . why disturb it?" A trustee who heads the investment committee at another school says, "I guess we'd have a consultation with the interested trustee before there was any sale just in case some upset would happen." He adds that he is not sure just what the policy would be because "I don't think we've ever tried to sell any of the sensitive stocks that have been given to the university."

In addition to accepting gifts, endowment funds often purchase trustee-linked stocks on the open market. At Washington and Northwestern universities, the endowment funds have acquired positions in companies with which members of the trustee investment committees were affiliated. Noting that the trustee involved always abstained from voting on the decision to buy or hold his own stock, the treasurer of one large college conceded, "You can't really blame them if sometimes they recommend each other's stock. After all, these people know each other very well."

Few trustees whose companies are represented in the endowment portfolios they supervise appear to have derived any significant financial benefit from the institution's holding. Open market buying on the scale of Washington's or Northwestern's purchases almost certainly had no readily discernible effect on the stocks' prices. The price effects of sales may be more significant. But even if Washington abruptly unloaded its 30,785 shares of Monsanto or 71,739 shares of McDonnell Douglas, the prices of the stocks would be affected at most very temporarily. And Northwestern could easily dispose of its 576,984 shares of American Hospital Supply (1.5 percent of the total outstanding) or Emory of its Coca-Cola holdings (also 1.5 percent) without permanently affecting stock prices by reducing its positions gradually or, in the case of securities unregistered with the SEC, selling them through a well-managed registered secondary offering. Endowment funds hold these positions not because the trustees are seeking to enrich themselves or to shore up their own portfolios but to make the trustee or donor feel good, to reinforce his ties with the school, to avoid embarrassing him. If a trustee-linked position were liquidated, the damage, if any, would be not to the trustee's portfolio but to his pride, and to his loyalty to the school.

Shareholder votes, especially those involving hostile tender offers or proxy fights, are more dangerous to the personal financial interests of trustees than simple buy or sell decisions. For the management of the company involved, a successful takeover can be tragic. Often many of the existing top managers are fired. For shareholders, though, the same situation can be a windfall. Outsiders making tender offers usually are willing to pay an attractive premium over the current market price; hence, if the offer is a success, shareholders enjoy a substantial capital gain. Shareholders also can benefit if a badly managed company is absorbed by a well-managed concern that installs a fresh group of executives.

The voting of large endowment fund blocks, such as Northwestern's 1.5 percent of American Hospital Supply or Swarthmore's 1.7 percent of Standard Pressed Steel, might be decisive in a closely contested takeover struggle. But endowment funds are unlikely to vote important trustee-linked blocks against management. Asked how he would feel if the university considered voting a large block of stock he had donated in favor of an unfriendly takeover aspirant, one trustee expresses astonishment at the proposition: "I would think that if they're interested in getting more contributions over the years," he says, "they would say to themselves, 'Let's not aggravate this guy by voting the stock the wrong way. Otherwise, he may not give us any more.' That's just common sense. Goddamn it, they don't get big chunks of stock from everybody."

Some corporate executives have used the technique of donating major blocks to colleges and universities both to keep the shares from being liquidated to pay estate taxes after their deaths and to secure for their families or chosen successors continued control of their respective companies. Galen J. Roush, co-founder of Roadway Express, Inc., and, until his death last year, a trustee of Hiram College in Ohio, donated a large block of Roadway Express to Hiram and made it the beneficiary of a nonvoting trust explicitly for that purpose. Members of Roush's family own 41.9 percent of the company's other shares. The trust and the shares the college owns directly make up 40 percent of its endowment.

Washington University has a one-third interest in a trust consisting of 1,534,344 shares of Mallinckrodt, Inc., a large drug and chemicals concern that was established by the late Edward Mallinckrodt, Jr. Before his death, Mallinckrodt appointed as trustees of this trust a number of the directors of his company; he further arranged for their trusteeship to end in 1982 and for the university to assume voting control at that time. According to Washington University treasurer Merl M. Huntsinger, "His whole idea was to avoid the possibility of a takeover" of the company he had founded. The trust in which Washington has an interest and another family trust constitute 24 percent of the company's stock. At the moment, Harold E. Thayer, Mallinckrodt's chief executive and a trustee for the trusts, is a trustee of Washington University. William H. Danforth, chancellor of the university, is a director of Mallinckrodt.

Gifts and bequests of major blocks for such purposes may be on the rise. At one time, the standard practice of corporate executives seeking to keep control stock in friendly hands was to establish private foundations.* But the Tax Reform Act of 1969 sharply reduced the usefulness of foundations as control mechanisms by imposing limits on the portion of a company's stock a foundation could hold. Now a foundation that receives a large block of stock generally must reduce it to no more than 20 percent of the company's outstanding shares within five years. This rule may divert the donation of control stock from foundations to other nonprofit institutions. According to John G. Simon, a professor at Yale Law School and the president of the Taconic Foundation: "[T]here are hundreds of thousands of financially hard-pressed colleges and churches

*See pp. 51–88.

which would be delighted to receive control stock with all kinds of informal voting understandings. . . . [T]here is evidence that such diversions are being actively solicited. . . ."[2]

Among its many drawbacks, the presence of large, trustee-linked blocks in a portfolio can increase investment risk by reducing diversification. The financial future of Emory University, for example, is closely linked to the continuing prosperity of Coca-Cola. "Coca-Cola has done very well over the years," says Francis Fenn of the National Association of College and University Business Officers, "but if the university had had all that money in Penn Central, it would have been tragic." The University of Rochester's endowment income, which supplied 17 percent of the school's revenues during 1975–76, could be materially affected by a major change in the fortunes of Kodak and Xerox. And in the past two years, these two stocks have lost much of the glamour that they had during the 1950s and 1960s. Although few universities hold such large blocks, many are heavily and probably excessively concentrated in companies within a small geographic region whose prosperity is vulnerable to shifts in, for example, government spending and demographic patterns. Still other schools are excessively concentrated in a single industry. Some 36 percent of the common stock portfolio of Rockefeller University, which is effectively controlled by the Rockefeller family, is invested in energy issues, principally Exxon Corp. The Rockefeller family, of course, has many ties to the energy industry.

Failure to diversify portfolio assets is regarded by nearly all investment experts and some courts as inherently imprudent. The trustee's duty to diversify, long an integral part of trust law, is codified in *Restatement of Trusts (Second)* as follows: "Except as otherwise provided by the terms of the trust, the trustee is under a duty to the beneficiary to distribute the risk of loss by a reasonable diversification of investments, unless under the circumstances it is prudent not to do so."[3] The Employee Retirement Income Security Act of 1974 imposed the duty to diversify investments on all pension trusts and other employee benefit plans covered by the act.[4] According to attorney Marion Fremont-Smith:

> One aspect of the application of the prudent man rule to trust departments is the question of diversification of risk. Common sense dictates that it is not prudent to keep too many eggs in one basket. The question of diversification is particularly important to trustees of the many charitable foundations to which donors have contributed large amounts of stock of a closely held corporation. Unfortunately, the cases do not make clear how far a trustee is subject

to liability for failure to diversify investments. The requirement for diversification has been specifically recognized by the courts in some jurisdictions and has been imposed by statute in others.[5]

It seems at least possible that failure to diversify could subject a school's trustees to legal challenge, especially if it could be shown that such failure jeopardized the endowment fund's assets.

Imprudent investments can affect the contributions of all a school's benefactors because most schools pool their endowment fund assets. When a new gift is received, it is added to the pool and credited with units or shares in the pool. The value of the gift then becomes the value of its shares, and like a mutual fund shareholder, the gift benefits on a pro rata basis from the return of the endowment fund as a whole. If a large, trustee-linked block performs badly, has a very low yield, or subjects the portfolio to excessive risk and volatility, all gifts, and their designated uses, from scholarships and professorships to student loans and libraries, will suffer accordingly.

Investment manager John W. Bristol, whose firm has several endowment clients, approaches the problem from a different perspective: "I think a little potential conflict of interest is not too much of a price to pay, considering the alternative of cutting off the golden goose." A badly performing, undiversified block of stock is after all better than no stock at all.

This counter-argument has merit. But it does not provide a blanket justification for golden-goose coddling and cozy trustee-portfolio relationships. College and university investment officers should confront the issue directly, weighing the dangers of a possibly risky, undiversified portfolio, the appearance of conflict-of-interest abuse, and the possibility of embarrassing criticism or even legal action against the hope of future donations and the chances that the golden goose would actually stop producing if his previous gifts were unloaded.

Some trustees make it very clear that they consider the donated block a "good investment" for the endowment and that it should be left alone. But as John W. Bristol notes: "Often the reluctance to sell is exaggerated because sometimes the donor couldn't care less." Both the University of Pittsburgh and Carnegie-Mellon University have disposed of substantial portions of Gulf Oil stock donated to them by members of the Mellon family, without causing noticeable concern to their benefactors. Unfortunately, the subject of abuses and problems resulting from trustee-linked stock positions comes up at all too few trustee meetings, either because no one thinks anything is wrong with the practice or because no one is willing to risk giving offense. Leigh A. Jones, vice-president for finance at Berea College in Kentucky, recalls the reluctance of some new investment firms he had hired as endowment fund managers to accept his assurances that a large holding in Ralston Purina Co. stock donated by Berea trustee Donald Danforth, Jr., whose family had founded the company, could be sold whenever the managers deemed it appropriate:

> We told the managers they had complete discretion, but it took them a while to get used to it. Once, one of the managers called me and said: "Leigh, what about the Ralston stock?" I said: "What about it? We told you you could do whatever you wanted with it." He said: "Do you really mean that? What happens if I sell it? Aren't I going to get in dutch?" Even though I said he wouldn't, I know that for a while at least the manager thought twice about coming before the investment committee with Danforth sitting across from him and explaining why he felt some of the stock should be sold.

Not all investment managers are timid. Hazel Sanger of Thorndike, Doran, Paine & Lewis reports that when her firm is confronted with a sensitive block: "We think it is our fiduciary obligation to point out to the trustees the risks of nondiversification or any specific risk in the company. Then if the trustees feel that despite the risks they want to hold the stock, then at least they have made an informed decision." If they decide to hold the stock, Thorndike segregates it in a special account away from the rest of the portfolio.

"You have to push trustees' noses into the [conflict-of-interest] question," says Columbia University professor Roger Murray. "They hope it'll go away or that you won't nag them about it." But if more investment managers confronted the trustees with the issue and more trustees and university officials took the trouble to analyze the advantages and disadvantages of holding such blocks, they might eliminate many of the existing abuses.

IV/Investment Managers, Brokers, and Bankers

At one point during the early 1960s, the board of trustees at a large New England university was looking for a full-time investment advisor. The trustees had run the endowment fund's portfolio themselves for many years, and although the treasurer and one or two of the more enlightened trustees had convinced the others that the time had come to secure the services of a well-qualified outside professional, the trustees refused to pay an advisor more than $6,000 per year. One of the trustees was assigned the difficult task of finding the right man for the job. After much searching, the trustee discovered a brilliant young analyst who hated New York, where he was then employed, loved the idea of working on a tree-shaded campus, and did not mind the low salary because his wife came from a very wealthy family. The trustees rejected the man because he had graduated from the university's traditional football rival.

In the last decade, universities have made substantial progress in eliminating intramural sports rivalries and other extraneous considerations from the selection of those who provide advisory, managerial, brokerage, and banking services to endowment funds. Today, for numerous colleges and universities, competence and cost are the only relevant criteria. Yet in too many instances, competence and cost receive lower priority than affiliation with trustees and prominent donors.

Investment Managers and Advisors

Perhaps the most visible change since the old days of management by crony has been the now common practice of hiring independent professional managers. In the past, the head of the investment committee often employed his own firm to manage the endowment. Today, numerous educational institutions give outside investment managers discretion to make portfolio investments subject only to broad policy guidelines. Despite its close ties to Nashville, for instance, Vanderbilt University divides up management of its $124 million endowment fund among four outside managers: Capital Guardian Trust Co. in Los Angeles; First National Bank of Chicago; Thorndike, Doran, Paine & Lewis in Atlanta; and United States Trust Co. in New York.

Ohio State University in Columbus, Ohio, which also is closely associated with its community, uses Thorndike in Atlanta and Alliance Capital Management Corp. in Minneapolis for its $49.3 million endowment. Several schools, including Harvard, the University of Chicago, the University of California, the University of Pennsylvania (which has completely reorganized and professionalized its investment staff since the Penn Central episode), and Syracuse, maintain a staff of in-house professionals who generally have discretion to make individual portfolio selections and are often advised by outside firms. The portfolios of these schools tend to be well-diversified assemblages of institutional grade securities largely free of trustee-linked aberrations and discernible conflicts of interest.

The internal management of such schools as Harvard operates with relatively little trustee involvement and, according to some treasurers, is cheaper, more efficient, and more responsive to the school's needs than outside management would be. But internal management can increase the risk of conflicts of interest. Both Northwestern University and the University of Rochester, where links between portfolio holdings and trustees are especially evident, are internally managed.

One of the advantages of paid professional management is that it can always be replaced if the portfolio's performance is unsatisfactory. Colleges and universities at which the members of the investment committee or merely of the board are closely involved in the portfolio's management have no such recourse. "What happens if the trustees flunk the test?" asks Hans H. Jenny of Wooster College. "Who's going to say you really goofed? I've seen this happen with many institutions I've consulted with. Nobody spanks Mama because she might leave you a million bucks. So you have to put up with a lot of bad or hands-off management just so you won't ruffle trustee feathers." The interests of the fund thus are subverted in order to avoid upsetting or embarrassing the involved trustees.

At a large number of schools, the job of managing the endowment is an apparent captive of one or more local institutions, usually banks, that are closely linked to the school and its board of trustees. At the University of Pittsburgh, the Mellon Bank manages most of the $88,913,454 in endowment assets (as of June 30, 1976); the Pittsburgh National Bank manages the rest. The Mellon family, which controls the bank, has been the university's most important donor. Of the university's twelve charter trustees, one is James H. Higgins, chairman of the board of Mellon National Corporation, the bank's holding company, and four more are directors of Mellon National Corporation. The board also includes Merle E. Gilliard, chairman of Pittsburgh National Bank, and two members of the board of his bank's holding company. Of the university's $43.9 million in current and loan funds and plant funds, $16.3 million is invested in Mellon National and Pittsburgh National securities. The endowment portfolios run by the two banks are relatively free of large holdings of securities linked to the university's trustees or Mellon interests. Nevertheless, as trustees and fiduciaries, the chairmen of Mellon Bank and Pittsburgh National Bank have apparently voted to award, or at least acquiesced in the award of, the management of the university's endowment fund to themselves. If the bank's most recently published fee schedule is applicable, during the fiscal year ending June 30, 1976, Mellon received approximately $65,000 for managing its portion of the university's portfolio.

Management of Case Western Reserve University's $82,990,247 in endowment and similar funds (as of June 30, 1976) is divided up among the Cleveland Trust Co., the National City Bank of Cleveland, and Central National Bank, the city's three major banks. The vice-chairman of Cleveland Trust and the chairman of National City Bank are on Case Western's boards of trustees and overseers. Eight corporations whose present or former officers are trustees of the university are also represented on the board of National City Bank. Case Western Reserve president Louis A. Toepfer and a Case Western professor are board members of CleveTrust Corp., the holding company for Cleveland Trust, as are three corporate executives who are also Case Western trustees. Several partners from Jones, Day, Reavis & Pogue, a powerful law firm closely associated with Cleveland industry, are trustees of the university and are on the boards of all three banks. A listing of stocks in Case Western's endowment portfolio (as of November 30, 1976) shows positions in National City Corp., CleveTrust Corp., and CleveTrust Realty Investors SBI, as well as in ten other companies whose executives are on the university's board of trustees. Most of these companies are located in Cleveland and have commercial and trust relationships with the three major local banks.

Emory University's endowment has one outside manager, Trust Company Bank of Atlanta, which also is a lender to the school. Emory's board includes no fewer than four present or former executives of the bank: Robert Strickland, chairman of the bank; William R. Bowdoin, head of the bank's executive committee; George S. Craft, former chairman of the bank; and James B. Williams, head of Trust Company of Georgia Associates, an affiliate of the bank. Three other directors of the bank are also trustees. The Trust Company Bank also has been very close to Coca-Cola ever since Ernest Woodruff, who formed the syndicate that bought control of the company in 1919, headed the bank. A former chairman of the bank, the current honorary chairman, and a director of Trust Company of Georgia, the bank's holding company, are on Coca-Cola's board of directors. J. Paul Austin, chairman of Coca-Cola, is on the bank's board. The bank is also manager of much of the Woodruff family money, including the $205 million Emily and Ernest Woodruff Foundation.

The University of Rochester is not the only school in that city with conflicting relationships. Rochester Institute of Technology's (RIT) $63,246,399 in endowment and similar funds (as of June 30, 1976) is managed by Lincoln First Bank of Rochester. Alexander D. Hargrave, chief executive of Lincoln First Banks, Inc., the holding company, is a trustee of RIT. Three other trustees or officers of RIT are directors of Lincoln First Banks, Inc. If Lincoln First Bank of Rochester's latest published fee schedule is applicable, the bank received about $55,000 for its services as manager during the past fiscal year.

At times, factors other than trustee affiliation can affect the direction of management business. The University of Minnesota, with an endowment of $83,085,349 (as of June 30, 1976) is a case in point. In the late 1960s, after many years of internal management, Roger Kennedy, then financial vice-president for the school and now vice-president of financial affairs at the Ford Foundation, organized a system of outside managers. The university's regents, who are appointed by the state legislature and are not usually important members of the local business establishment, had no objection. But D. P. Benda, manager of investment and cash management for the university, recalls being under "an awful lot of political pressure, particularly by the state legislators, to avoid managers from outside the state of Minnesota." Kennedy selected T. Rowe Price Associates from Baltimore; Thorndike, Doran, Paine & Lewis from Atlanta; Brokaw Capital Management from New York; Alliance Capital Management, headquartered in New York but with an office in Minneapolis; and—the sole local manager—Northwestern National Bank in Minneapolis, of which Roger Kennedy had been a director.

The state legislators were irate. In 1971, Brokaw Capital Management, whose performance had been below that of the other out-of-state firms, was fired and replaced by First Trust Company of St. Paul and Investment Advisors, Inc., of Minneapolis. As a result, the endowment now has three local and three out-of-state managers (if Alliance is counted as a New York firm), and the legislators are somewhat appeased. But the outsiders currently manage over 80 percent of the endowment fund.

Many treasurers of endowment funds, although unhappy that the management of the fund is an apparent captive of local institutions, assume that the relationship is too strong to be broken. Yet the possibility of change may be greater than they realize. For example, for many years, Carnegie-Mellon University in Pittsburgh used the Mellon Bank and Pittsburgh National Bank to run an endowment that amounted to $110,488,584 (as of June 30, 1976). On the surface, the management of this fund appeared to be as locked up as that of the University of Pittsburgh. The Mellons, of course, are heavy donors to Carnegie-Mellon. In addition, Donald C. Burnham, former chief executive of Westinghouse Electric Corp. and chairman of Carnegie-Mellon's board of trustees, and John D. Harper, former president of the Aluminum Co. of America and vice-chairman of the board of trustees, are both directors of Mellon National Corp.

In 1975, however, treasurer George O. Luster and other university officials succeeded in switching a major portion of their endowment assets to four new managers: Capital Guardian Trust in Los Angeles; Delaware Investment Advisors in Philadelphia; and F. Eberstadt & Co. and Fischer, Francis, Trees & Watts in New York. "The only way you can overcome reluctance to change," Luster says, "is to put forth your argument in a logical fashion supported by documentation that change is necessary." The argument Luster used in presenting the plan to the trustees was "risk diversification," the usefulness of dividing up the portfolio among different managers with different philosophies. According to Luster's latest report:

> The diversification of management philosophy and risk proved to be of substantial benefit in the first year of operation. The investment performance of the equity manager group exceeded the return achieved by the Standard & Poor's 500 Index without any loss in quality and with a decrease in the volatility of the portfolio.

Quite likely at other institutions as well, the apparently very close links between universities and their endowment fund managers are more the product of tradition and inertia than of active, self-interested efforts by trustees affiliated with the managers to perpetuate a profitable captive relationship. Perhaps if presented with persuasive reasons why a change would be beneficial, trustees would be willing to go along.

Trustees may be less willing to go along with the idea of putting some or all of their endowment assets in "index funds," which have been widely discussed in the investment business in recent years.[1] The idea derives from the notion, elaborately documented in statistical studies, that the stock market is "efficient"—that the price of each stock accurately reflects all publicly available information about the stock's future as well as investors' feelings and opinions about it. If the stock market is indeed efficient, in this sense, it is virtually impossible, except through luck, to assemble a portfolio of securities that will consistently outperform the market as a whole. Academicians have long advanced this theory,[2] but it did not begin to gain acceptance in the investment world until a large number of studies of the performance of actual institutional portfolios revealed that, over time, few outperformed such broadly based market indices as the Standard & Poor's 500.

Index funds do not try to beat the market. They merely seek to match it or, more accurately, to match the S&P 500 or one of the other widely followed indices, by assembling portfolios of all or most of the stocks in the index they are trying to evaluate. Such index funds outperform most conventionally managed portfolios, whose performance is weighted down by the heavy costs, in brokerage commissions and research, of trying to beat the market. The cost advantage of index funds over conventionally managed portfolios is compelling. Batterymarch Financial Corp., a Boston investment manager that offers index services, publishes an annual estimated relative cost comparison for management of a $25 million fund. Index funds have negligible turnover—just 2 or 3 percent to compensate for changes in the index. Hence, the brokerage commissions on $25 million would be $2,500 if the money were in an index fund or $53,000 if it were in a portfolio whose managers were continually buying and selling securities in their efforts to achieve high performance. The administrative costs of index funds are very low because they require no investment research; Batterymarch's management fee for running the $25 million portfolio would be $25,000, as against $154,000 for a conventional manager, who would need to pay a large staff of analysts and buy outside research and statistical services. Batterymarch also claims to save additional money in trading costs because, unlike active managers, it does not tend to chase the same groups of stocks up and down at the same time. Batterymarch calculates the total annual cost of managing $25 million as $61,500 under indexing and $438,000 under conventional management.

Impressed by these cost comparisons, pension fund trustees, including those for such major corporations as AT&T, Exxon, and Ford, have invested some $2 billion in index funds to date. According to some Wall Street estimates, the figure could be $10 billion in a couple of years.[3]

Although no college or university is known to have invested its endowment money in index funds, many school treasurers, unhappy with the cost and performance of conventional managers, are attracted by the idea.[4] According to a survey conducted by the National Association of College and University Business Officers (NACUBO), for the ten years ending June 30, 1976, the seventy-seven participating pooled endowments achieved an average annual return of 3.71 percent; the S&P 500 received an average annual return of 4.70 percent.[5] "I'm kind of enamored with [index funds] at this point," says Leigh Jones of Berea College. "If you're a long-term investor like a college, where you're looking ahead 25 or 50 years, maybe it's the best route to go." But Jones admits, "I'd have a hard time selling my board or my finance committee." The chairman of Berea's finance committee is Kroger Pettengill, former president of the First National Bank of Cincinnati and now head of an investment counseling firm. Nearly all conventional money managers are opposed, often heatedly, to index funds. "Maybe if you're a money manager," says Jones, "it's like being a gambler. You keep thinking, I can do it, I can win."

Numerous experts with less of a vested interest than conventional money managers still argue that superior performance can be achieved. "Let's agree that only one out of ten managers consistently outperforms the averages after transaction costs," says Roger Murray of Columbia:

> If you're lazy or incompetent and you don't know how to find the manager who can deliver superior performance, then use an index fund. But if you're not and if you think your responsibility is to maximize the productivity of the endowment fund, don't accept a second-best solution. Go to work and find the one out of ten. There is no question in my mind it can be done. I've done it myself enough times.

Given the apparent cost savings, though, college and university trustees may have to consider index funds seriously, especially if they have an affiliation with the existing manager of the endowment fund. J. Peter Williamson, professor at the Amos Tuck School of Business Administration at Dartmouth and an expert on endowment funds, says:

> It may not be too long before college and university trustees will be in trouble if they have not explicitly considered index funds and made a decision for or against them with evidence to support that decision. That doesn't mean that it is imprudent not to go into an index fund. But prudence demands that you

have to have at least looked into it. And if your own performance has been below the level of an index fund, you had better be prepared to explain why you prefer your own managers to an index fund.

Rejecting index funds out of hand may come to be regarded as a conflict-of-interest abuse, a case of the trustee pursuing his own vested interest in perpetuating the fund's relationship with a manager with which he is affiliated, or simply protecting his own uninformed prejudices and preconceptions rather than the interests of the endowment fund and, as a result, costing the endowment fund money it otherwise might not have had to spend.

Brokers

It has long been a common practice in the investment business to use brokerage commissions to pay for numerous other services besides execution of stock and bond transactions. Some of the services, such as research, are relatively legitimate. Others, such as a quid pro quo paid by trust departments for deposits by brokers,[6] raise serious questions.

Colleges and universities commonly use commissions to reward trustees and donors for their services—most often, apparently, because the trustees and donors demand them. "The pressure is very, very heavy, and I don't see it ever relenting," says Roger Murray of Columbia. "There are a lot of alumni who will be absolutely open about it. For every dollar of commission business they receive, they say they will make a contribution of fifty cents."

Investment manager John W. Bristol adds: "There have been more abuses in this area than any other. Alumni at brokerage houses are always crying to the treasurer, talking about how generous they are during annual giving. Trustees feel it is important to support alumni at brokerage houses who are or could be potential givers." For many years at one southern university, the head of the trustees' investment committee insisted that all the commission business be sent to his own brokerage firm. Although some of the other trustees complained, he maintained he could do the business as well as anyone else.

Many treasurers strive to resist such pressures from alumni and donors. "The problem comes up, but we duck it," says Leigh Jones of Berea. "We tell people we've given the authority to the managers and that they handle the brokerage." Other treasurers admit to going along. Merl M. Huntsinger, treasurer of Washington University, reports that he and the trustees give the three local banks and two investment firms who manage the endowment fund "guidelines" on how the commission business should be allocated:

> We tell them, all things being equal, these are the brokers we want you to use. We tell them to spread it around in accordance with the weighting we give them. The list is put together from people who work with us in various ways. For instance, there is one small local firm who gave an endowed professorship a few years ago, and needless to say he is close to our hearts. So we remember him when we have some brokerage business that his firm can do. It's this type of thing: people who work with us, who are members of the investment committee, or people who help the university raise funds or who are substantial contributors.

(The member of the investment committee to whom Huntsinger was apparently referring is Elliot H. Stein, president of Scherck, Stein & Franc, Inc., a small, St. Louis-based brokerage house.) Northwestern has sent commission business to brokerage houses represented on its board, including Smith Barney, Harris Upham & Co., Dean Witter & Co., and First of Michigan Corp.

This practice can lead to some rather blatant abuses. One investment manager tells of a southwestern college that was considering switching management of its endowment fund from a local bank, which had performed poorly, to a New York investment counselor. The move was vetoed by partners at three local brokerage houses who are members of the board of trustees. They were enjoying most of the fund's commission business and felt that they might not receive the same consideration from the New York house, which had a policy of not accepting brokerage direction from clients.

A respected endowment executive claims firsthand knowledge of an instance involving a college trustee whose bank handled a major part of the college's $30 million endowment. The bank churned the account vigorously and in one year generated for itself $200,000 in commissions, much of it for unnecessary transactions. The accountant for the fund brought the unnecessary transactions to the attention of the school's president. But he declined to take action because the trustee was one of the school's largest donors.

Few trustees would condone such churning. Yet, according to John W. Bristol, many trustees have the "misguided belief" that merely spreading commissions around to the firms of donors and similarly deserving parties is harmless. This belief stems in part from the fact that, prior to May 1, 1975, the brokerage commissions charged by members of the New York Stock Exchange and other exchanges were fixed. Cheaper executions often could be obtained in the "third market," the over-the-counter market in issues listed on the Big Board. But the third market, in part thanks to NYSE propaganda, was regarded as somewhat illicit. Investors who wanted to deal with a "reputable" NYSE firm had to pay the fixed rate. Since all NYSE members charged the same rate, the reasoning went, why not send the orders to the university's friends?

Investment houses vary considerably in execution ability, however. Few small regional firms of the sort most likely to be receiving commissions from an endowment fund due to trustee or donor ties can match the ability of the major New York firms, particularly in handling large blocks. If using a local firm costs an endowment fund only a quarter of a point in unloading a 5,000 share position, the school loses $1,250.

In any case, on May 1, 1975, fixed rates were abolished and brokerage commissions became competitive. By the end of 1976, price competition had become fierce, and some firms were offering discounts as high as 70 to 80 percent off the old rate.[7] Discounts vary widely from firm to firm, and from customer to customer. To a large extent, the customers who bargain the most vigorously pay the lowest commissions. Endowment funds do not release breakdowns of the commissions they pay by amounts and recipients. But it seems reasonable to assume that endowment funds generally receive smaller discounts from local firms headed by a trustee or loyal alumnus than they would from the 70-percent-off "deep discounters," as the firms are called. If the trustee's firm gives only a 20 percent discount, a major portion of the commission the endowment fund pays is not an unavoidable payment that might otherwise go to a firm unconnected with the school but simply a reward for the trustee's loyalty or generosity. The available evidence indicates that very few people who oversee endowment funds have ever actually weighed the contributions or services received against the added commission costs. If a university receives $2,500 in donations from a loyal alumnus and pays his firm $5,000 in unnecessary commission business, the relationship costs the university $2,500 and subjects it to the potential embarrassment of engaging in a practice that, if not exactly illegal, is certainly questionable as well as unfair to donors or trustees who do not happen to be in the brokerage business. Hazel Sanger of Thorndike, Doran, Paine & Lewis says that her firm requires trustees to supply in writing all brokerage instructions not predicated on best price or best execution. In such cases, she reports, "we make sure the trustees know what kinds of discounts are available elsewhere so that they can assess the competitiveness of the brokers they want us to use. If they choose to direct brokerage on a noncompetitive basis for what they may consider the broader interests of their institution, at least they will have made an informed decision."

Bankers

Custodianship of investment securities and other banking services can be a major cost to endowment funds and thus a major area for cost savings. According to J. Peter Williamson, professor at Dartmouth's Amos Tuck School of Business Administration:

> Selecting a custodian calls for a careful comparison of costs, services, and quality of service among candidates. The best assurance that the present custodian fees and services are appropriate, of course, will come from "shopping around." The bank and custodial arrangements and the level of efficiency in an institution's handling of cash call for regular evaluation. The sums of money at stake can be quite substantial compared with the income on the endowment.[8]

Instead of permitting large non-interest-bearing cash balances to build up at its bank, the managers of an endowment fund should keep these balances as low as possible and keep the fund's cash constantly at work in the most productive way. Instead of permitting the custodian to accumulate dividends and interest for days or weeks before crediting them to the endowment fund, managers should make sure that this money is credited on settlement day. Many colleges and universities work assiduously to obtain the best banking and custodian services at the lowest price. Many manage their cash as efficiently as large corporations. Harvard, which has put a great deal of study into obtaining the most efficient banking services, maintains no balances at commercial banks. But a number of other schools have long-standing arrangements with trustee-linked banks for the usual reasons and with predictable results. According to Williamson, bank relationships are the most important single area of conflict-of-interest problems at endowment funds:

> The way it works—and this is on the basis of talking to quite a few people who have explored it—is that you have the president or chairman of the local bank on your board of trustees. It is not the trustee deliberately having the college maintain excessive balances. It is the financial officer of the college thinking he could get a better deal for the college, but being very reluctant to go to the bank and say either you give us a better deal or we'll switch banks. Instead, he decides not to make a fuss because it would upset the college's relationship with the trustee, who may be a big donor. Colleges and universities have been very slow in getting the best banking services and the reason is that it is often not very comfortable for them to do so. It's not comfortable to get tough with someone who is on your board of trustees.

Colleges and universities do not disclose the terms of their banking relationships. But in case after case, the custodian for an endowment fund, and thus quite possibly the school's commercial bank as well, also manages the endowment fund and has a representative on the board of trustees. Case Western Reserve's custodians are the same three Cleveland banks that manage the fund and are linked to the board of trustees. Washington University's custodians are the four St. Louis banks that manage its fund and are represented on its board. The custodian banks for the University of Rochester's endowment fund are Central Trust Company, Lincoln First Bank, and Security Trust Company. The chief executives of all three banks are trustees of the university. In such circumstances, trustees are apparently voting or acquiescing in the allocation of business from the trust for which they are fiduciaries to institutions with which they are affiliated.

These universities may be receiving excellent, low-cost service from their banks. Perhaps the banker on the board even directs his bank to give the school a cut-rate price. But in most cases, the university is a captive customer. Logic suggests that a tough customer, inclined to shop around, may receive better service than a docile, captive customer.

The extent to which schools are the captives of local or trustee-linked banks has become apparent through the experiences of the Common Fund, a nonprofit cooperative endeavor that offers several pooled investment vehicles specifically designed for educational institutions. The Common Fund, which began operations in 1971 with the aid of a Ford Foundation grant, has not been so successful in attracting assets as its organizers had expected.

The failure of many schools to invest in the Common Fund's equity vehicle may be due in part to its disappointing performance. But nearly everybody agrees that the performance and structure of the Common Fund's pooled cash management vehicle, the Common Fund for Short Term Investments, has been extremely good. It provides participants with an elaborate wire transfer mechanism that allows them to make immediate additions and withdrawals. Shortly after the fund was established in 1974, George F. Keane, executive director for the Common Fund, estimated that colleges and universities had close to $5 billion in liquid assets, which potentially could be invested in the fund.[9] Yet by the end of 1976, the fund had attracted only slightly more than $50 million.

"The whole concept [of the short-term fund] is working out beautifully, just as well as we had hoped," says Roger Murray of Columbia, who is a Common Fund trustee:

It is a very effective device for managing cash and keeping balances to a minimum level. But we're not getting the volume and the activity. If you ask a treasurer why he doesn't participate, he'll say, well, we already have a pretty good system, or we already watch our balances. But you can't help but think that it is partly due to his unwillingness to create problems with his local banker who is a trustee. There is a certain tightness about these local relationships. The treasurer doesn't want to let go of the money. He doesn't want those relationships reduced. In the development of the Common Fund, this is a problem we've run into repeatedly.

The treasurer of a West Coast college reports that his recent proposal for participation in the Common Fund's short-term fund was vetoed by two local bankers who were trustees of the school and handled the school's banking business.

For many years, a local bank had been investment advisor and custodian of the endowment fund of The College of Wooster in Ohio. When Hans H. Jenny, Wooster's vice-president for finance, expressed dissatisfaction with the quality of service and proposed to switch, he ran into intense opposition from three trustees. One was an accountant whose firm handled the local bank and who was on the local bank's board. Another was an officer of a large bank of which the small bank was a correspondent. The third, as Jenny put it, "was just miffed because we were violating a long historical relationship." The bank officer and the traditionalist had been important donors; in protest, they stopped giving. But Jenny's biggest problem was with the accountant. "We had a terrible hassle with him," Jenny recalls. "When the administration came up with proposals for switching banks, he said, 'We can always find new administrators.' " When the college finally chose a new bank, the accountant resigned from the board of trustees. The other two trustees remained and eventually began making donations again. But making the switch and "establishing peace on the board," says Jenny, "took three and a half years."

V/Conclusions

Incestuous relationships, apparent self-dealing, and other conflicts of interest remain widespread at educational institutions mainly because many trustees see nothing wrong in them. Yet over the years to come, these practices may become grounds for legal action and, as a result, the focus of growing public criticism. Much attention, in this regard, is being focused on an important 1974 court case involving the Sibley Memorial Hospital, a nonprofit institution in Washington, D.C., with about $5 million in assets.[1] According to one commentator, the case

> presents for the first time an exhaustive review of the legal standards of care to be exercised by trustees of nonprofit organizations. It is a landmark decision and one which is being studied carefully by trustees and legal counsels of nonprofit organizations.[2]

The five defendants in the Sibley case were trustees and members of the hospital's investment committee as well as officers or directors of local financial institutions. The charges, brought by the hospital's patients in a class action, involved conspiracy, mismanagement, nonmanagement, and self-dealing. The self-dealing charges entailed a clear conflict of interest: the hospital did considerable business with the institutions with which the trustees were affiliated. The relationships included non-interest-bearing demand deposits, a mortgage loan, and an investment advisory contract. Two of the defendants were officers and directors of two local banks. The hospital's checking account had alternated between those two banks. In the year before suit was brought, the account held about $1 million, more than one-third of the hospital's investable funds, an amount that District Judge Gerhard A. Gesell found not justified by the defendants, although he also found that the plaintiffs had not established that the practice was "the result of a conscious direction on the part of" the interlocked directors who were the defendants.

In addition, Judge Gesell found that each of the defendants had "breached his fiduciary duty to supervise the management of Sibley's investments."[3] Although noting that District of Columbia law, like that of most jurisdictions, does not bar trustees from placing funds under their control in banks with which they are affiliated, the judge said the defendants had failed to disclose adequately to other persons involved in approving the transactions their outside interests or their knowledge of better terms available elsewhere. In some cases, including the awarding of an investment advisory contract to Ferris & Co., whose chairman and principal stockholder, George Ferris, was a trustee, the defendants had participated in or voted in favor of decisions to transact business with their own firms.

Because the hospital did not thereby suffer any measurable injury and because the defendants had neither engaged in actually fraudulent practices nor profited personally from their actions, Judge Gesell did not rule that they were financially liable. Nor did he approve the plaintiffs' requests for such injunctive relief as removal of the defendants as trustees and an absolute ban on dealings between the hospital and firms with which any of its trustees had an affiliation. He noted that the hospital had recently adopted a new bylaw based on new conflict-of-interest guidelines issued by the American Hospital Association.[4] However, he did decree, among other measures, strict rules for disclosure by trustees of outside affiliations.

Although the remedies he chose were modest, Gesell also included in his decision a strongly worded and subsequently widely read passage on the hiring of new trustees by the hospital:

The tendency of representatives of [financial institutions joining the board] is often to seek business in return for advice and assistance rendered as trustees. It must be made absolutely clear that Board membership carries no right to preferential treatment in the placement or handling of the Hospital's investments or business accounts. The Hospital would be well advised to restrict membership on its Board to the representatives of financial institutions which have no substantial business relationship with the Hospital. The best way to avoid potential conflicts of interest and to be assured of objective advice is to avoid the possibility of such conflicts at the time new trustees are selected.[5]

According to Charles T. Stewart, general counsel for J. C. Penney Co. and a trustee of Cornell University, the precedent set by the Sibley Hospital case should dispel the "sense of euphoria" that trustees of educational institutions have "probably had . . . as a result of the absence of specific beneficiaries to whom the trustees were accountable." [6] In an earlier decision in the same case,[7] Judge Gesell found that the patients of Sibley Hospital had standing to bring a class action against the trustees on the grounds of a breach of trust; that decision, Stewart said, "indicates that college and university trustees should be concerned about being held accountable under certain circumstances to students, faculty, employees, or even alumni."[8]

In a recent interview, Stewart elaborated on this point:

There are a lot of people who don't think this is a serious problem. But I'm convinced it is. If you have a situation where the endowment fund has a terrible experience in the stock market, while at the same time enrollment is down and the school has to raise tuition 25 percent, and on the board of trustees you have some serious conflicts of interest, it's not impossible that a student or group of students would sue, and I think they would have standing to sue.

A group of benefactors also might bring a class action, charging that, by imprudently holding on to a large block of trustee-donated stock whose performance or yield had been inadequate, the managers and trustees of the endowment fund, due to pooling, had caused the value of the donors' bequests to decline. "There are potentially dozens of cases [like the Sibley Hospital case] lurking around [among endowment funds]," says Daniel Robinson, a partner with the accounting firm of Peat, Marwick, Mitchell, Inc., who oversees his firm's nonprofit clients:

This is a litigious society, and I don't think educational institutions will remain exempt from that kind of activity. As soon as you have a suit against trustees where the plaintiff collects some money, a good piece of change, you'll see five hundred of those cases in the next three years.

Several possible courses of action are open to trustees and educational administrators seeking to protect themselves from lawsuits and public criticism and to reduce the still wide prevalence of conflicts of interest:

1. **A total ban on conflicting relationships.** Judge Gesell's opinion implies that such a ban may be advisable. And some institutions have chosen this course. As a result of local publicity several years ago about

business dealings between the University of Minnesota and firms in which regents held stock, the University of Minnesota is not permitted to invest its endowment assets in any company in which a regent owns an interest, even though the university gives complete discretion to outside managers in the selection of portfolio securities.

The Common Fund has a formal conflict-of-interest policy that, among other things, prohibits any trustee or fund officer from having an affiliation with or interest in any investment manager, custodian bank, or securities firm with which the Common Fund does business. The fund has issued a policy statement specifying that "each affected person should avoid interests of any kind which, in the performance of any services for the Corporation or the Fund, might in fact or in appearance divert him from continued loyalty to the Corporation and the Fund." Because the Common Fund gives its investment managers discretion, in most cases, this policy does not prohibit trustees and officers of the fund from owning the same securities owned by the fund.

A total ban has certain disadvantages, according to Charles T. Stewart of J. C. Penney and Cornell:

> [I]t is questionable whether a college or university board should restrict its membership to representatives of financial institutions which have no substantial business relationships with the institution.
>
> The effect of such a requirement would be to eliminate from potential board membership a number of persons whose business experience, ability, and financial capacity would enable them to make important contributions of expertise and money to the institution or, conversely, to require the institution to do business only with second-rate investment and financial organizations.[9]

This view is perhaps overstated, except perhaps for very small colleges in very small communities. Most endowment funds may obtain satisfactory service from any of dozens of investment advisors, banks, and brokers that would not present conflicts with existing trustees. And yet the close network of relationships between universities, their communities, local businesses and financial institutions, and major donors may also provide very valuable nourishment to a university. Moreover, a contract between an endowment fund and an institution whose chief executive is on the board of trustees is not necessarily unfair or inequitable, although it is more likely than a contract with a nonaffiliated manager to be so. Finally, the evidence suggests that many apparent conflict-of-interest abuses are the result of timidity or eagerness to please on the part of the officers of the educational institution rather than the venality of the trustees. Of course, in some cases, trustees have approved of actions benefiting institutions with which they were affiliated. But the most serious self-dealing activities in the Sibley Hospital case were initiated by the hospital's treasurer, who apparently felt a personal obligation to favor institutions represented on the board.

Not all institutions are likely to find it necessary or possible to adopt a total ban on conflicts without undue inconvenience and disturbance of valuable relationships. But complete avoidance of conflicting relationships is a goal toward which all educational institutions should strive.

2. **A prohibition on voting on questions involving an outside institution with which one has an affiliation or interest.** Judge Gesell stated flatly: "The trustee of a charitable hospital should always avoid active participation in a transaction in which he or a corporation with which he is associated has a significant interest."[10]

But is this prohibition by itself sufficient protection? William C. Porth, general counsel for New York University, has stated:

> Over the years we have had officers or directors of major New York banks and trust companies on the University's board of trustees including some from institutions which handled major portions of our financial transactions. We can perceive no objection to this relationship provided always that any such trustee would not participate in any board decision which might present a possible conflict. Neither should there be any inhibition concerning ordinary business transactions between the institution and a firm with which a trustee is connected provided the trustee does not improperly influence such activities.[11]

Northwestern University also has an informal policy to the same effect. Yet as that school's portfolio holdings suggest, the members of some boards have close personal and business relationships and are unlikely to vote to fire a firm associated with a friend. A voting ban in itself is not necessarily a panacea against conflict-of-interest problems, although it is obviously better than nothing at all.

3. **Formal affirmation of a strict policy of avoiding conflict-of-interest improprieties.** After noting the problem of interest conflicts at nonprofit institutions and considering a complete prohibition on self-dealing situations, the Commission on Private Philanthropy and Public Needs recommended:

> that all tax-exempt organizations be required by law to maintain "arm's length" business relationships with profit-making organizations or activities in which any member of the organization's staff, any board member, or any ma-

jor contributor has a substantial financial interest, either directly or through his or her family[12]

Educational endowments should seriously consider putting themselves formally on record against any but arm's-length relationships. They should adopt strict procedures requiring disclosure by trustees to other trustees of relevant outside affiliations. If the trustees choose to do business with an organization with which a trustee has an affiliation, the record should clearly show that alternatives were carefully considered, that the selection was in the best business interests of the fund, and that the interested trustee did not participate in the decision.

4. **Public disclosure.** Trustees and endowment fund officers could go a long way toward establishing their concern for avoiding improprieties and toward curbing the temptation to engage in questionable practices if they broadened their standards of public disclosure. The investments and investment policies of an educational endowment fund are not a private matter. Given the numerous groups of people who are affected by the activities of a typical college or university, anything short of complete financial disclosure is unjustifiable. A comprehensive financial report should include the following items:

The affiliations of trustees. Most major corporations disclose the business and professional affiliations of their directors in annual reports. Many even list directors' outside board memberships. Most colleges and universities do not routinely disclose this information, and several even refused requests by the author for it. In addition, members of the trustees' finance or investment committees should be identified.

Portfolio investments. Some schools release detailed breakdowns of their portfolios, but most do not. Publication of this information and the list of trustee affiliations would make relationships between the two easy to spot and might inhibit trustee-linked investments.

The identity of investment managers and bank custodians. A few schools disclose this information. The University of Minnesota, the University of Pittsburgh, and Lawrence University, among others, even publish portfolio lists for each of the managers of their portfolio. But most do not. Schools also should disclose their broad investment objectives and philosophies and the degree of discretion given outside managers.

Fund performance. Most major colleges and universities now follow the reporting standards of the *Industry Audit Guide: Audits of Colleges and Universities,* which was prepared in 1973 by the Committee of the American Institute of Certified Public Accountants on College and University Accounting and Auditing. According to the *Audit Guide,* "The financial statements or notes should set forth the total performance (i.e., yield and gains or losses) of the investment portfolio based on cost and market value."[13] Yet too many schools still do not provide enough information to indicate to the reader how well the school's endowment fund has performed.[14] All should.

Conflict-of-interest relationships. Schools should disclose all trustee affiliations with or substantial stock interests in investment managers, brokerage houses, custodians, or banks that receive endowment fund business. Such disclosure is basically what Judge Gesell required of the hospital in the Sibley Hospital case. Charles T. Stewart, in his capacity as a Cornell University trustee, is working on a conflict-of-interest policy that would require trustees to make public disclosure of substantial stock holdings and outside directorships. In 1975, the American Institute of Certified Public Accountants published a policy statement on the disclosure of "related party transactions," requiring the reporting entity to release information on relationships whose effect is to prevent one of the parties "from fully pursuing its own separate interests."[15] According to Daniel Robinson of Peat, Marwick, Mitchell, this requirement may be applicable to relationships of the trustees of educational institutions with investment advisors, brokers, and banks with which the institution does business and to portfolio holdings in companies in which a trustee has a very large personal stock interest.

Accounting firms, however, have apparently been very slow to apply this policy to their audits of colleges and universities. Although the AICPA statement became effective for reports on periods ending on or after December 26, 1975, very few school financial reports for periods after this date disclose this information.

Disclosure, of course, is no panacea. But it could still go a long way toward reducing the still prevalent conflicts of interest and associated abuses at college and university endowment funds.

Foundations

VI/Introduction

In 1961, Wright Patman (D.-Tex.) stood up on the floor of the House of Representatives and declared:

> I am . . . concerned with, first, foundation-controlled businesses competing with small businesses; second, the economic effect of great amounts of wealth accumulating in privately-controlled, tax-exempt foundations; third, the problem of control of that capital for an undetermined period—in some instances perpetuity—by a few individuals or their self-appointed successors; and fourth, the foundation's power to interlock and knot together through investments, a network of commercial alliances, which assures harmonious action whenever they have a common interest. . . .[1]

Thus, Patman and his Select House Committee on Small Business began a historic eight-year fight against private foundations. Foundations have always been the richest of the nation's nonprofit institutions, subsisting not on donations from the general public but on the income from sometimes mammoth endowments created by bequests from wealthy donors. According to the latest edition of the authoritative *Foundation Directory*, published by the Foundation Center, 2,504 foundations in the United States each have assets of over $1 million. The assets of these foundations, as of reporting periods during 1972–73, totaled $31,497,000,000. The 22,421 foundations with assets of under $1 million apiece had total assets of $2,599,410,000.[2]

When Patman began his investigation, foundations were remarkably free to do whatever they liked with this wealth. To maintain their tax-exempt status, foundations had only to adhere to the very vague and

53

broad general requirement, set forth in Section 501 (c) (3) of the Internal Revenue Code, that they be "organized and operated exclusively for religious, charitable, scientific, testing for public safety, literary, or educational purposes, or for the prevention of cruelty to children or animals. . . ." Foundation trustees were even more autonomous than the trustees of educational endowments and other nonprofit institutions. Depending on the donor's expressed wishes, foundation boards could set criteria for the recipients of foundation funds and alter the criteria at will. They could spend as much or as little as they wanted. And unlike colleges and universities, which are inevitably the focus of public attention, foundations were able to operate, if they wished, in almost total secrecy. Even the Internal Revenue Service (IRS) accorded them only cursory attention. To a large extent, the tax exemption that foundations and other nonprofit institutions enjoy is subsidized by taxpayers, who must bear an additional financial burden to compensate for the taxes that foundations and their donors avoid. Yet foundations conducted themselves as if they were wholly private organizations to which no outsider need be given access.

In the absence of constraints, it was, perhaps, almost inevitable that abuses should develop. Section 501 (c) (3) provides, among other things, that "no part of the net earnings" of a foundation can inure "to the benefit of any private shareholder or individual." In six voluminous reports, packed with data and prefaced by often vituperative (but not always accurate) recitations of specific examples, Patman and his staff asserted that this provision had been violated regularly and on a very broad scale.[3]

The most dramatic of the instances cited by Patman were conflict-of-interest abuses deriving from extensive and incestuous linkages between foundations, donors, and companies with which donors were associated. In many cases, the linkages were so intimate and complex that it was impossible to tell where one facet of the relationship left off and another began. Whatever the arrangement, the common theme was near-exclusive dedication of the foundation to the financial interests of the donor and his company, with the interests of charity running at best a poor second. Self-dealing was widespread. Foundations made loans to the donor or his company at low or no interest rates, purchased assets from interested parties at excessively high prices, sold assets for excessively low prices, and made grants to the donor's friends and family. They participated in elaborate kickback schemes with the donor and his associates, paid high salaries to the donor's friends and relatives for services as foundation trustees, and subsidized the donor's personal living expenses.

More broadly, the Patman material illustrated the widespread use of the foundation mechanism as a combination tax-free private bank and holding company for donors. Having given a foundation a large block of his company's stock, a donor could deduct the stock's market value from his taxable income as a charitable contribution and avoid capital gains taxes on the stock's appreciation. Then he would install himself, his family, and his friends as trustees. Thus, he could retain control of the block and his company while using the foundation's assets to promote his own and his company's fortunes. Foundations were not required to pay taxes on the dividends and interest they received or on the appreciation of their portfolios. Apart from channeling an occasional token grant to charity, foundations were an ideal device for storing enormous accumulations of resources to be employed in accordance with the donors' wishes. When the donors died, control of foundations and their assets passed smoothly to their heirs and chosen successors without the inconvenience of estate taxes; thus, foundations provided a means of perpetuating family dynasties and corporate power.

During the late 1960s, public outrage at the activities of foundations reached a crescendo. The publication of Patman's reports coincided with growing concern, on the part of liberals, over the inequities of the tax laws in general and, on the part of conservatives, over revelations of leftist tendencies in the grant programs of several foundations, especially the giant Ford Foundation. And everybody was upset by disclosures that foundation funds were being used to corrupt public officials. The discovery that Justice Abe Fortas, for instance, had accepted an annual fee from a foundation controlled by Louis E. Wolfson, a stock manipulator under federal indictment, led to Fortas' resignation from the Supreme Court.

Aggressive foundation lobbying defeated some of the most stringent of Patman's proposed measures, including a Senate Finance Committee amendment that would have forced foundations to dispose of all their assets after forty years or pay a regular corporate income tax. But the Tax Reform Act of 1969 was far from toothless. It subjected private foundations to stiff controls, many of them specifically designed to curb conflicts of interest. The act defines private foundations as organizations other than churches, schools, and hospitals that are covered by Section 501 (c) (3) and receive more than a third of their support from investment income. The Internal Revenue Service enforces the provisions of the act, penalizing violators, in most instances, by means of excise taxes—an initial tax upon discovery of the violation and a much higher tax if the violation is not remedied within a prescribed period. The provisions of the act deal with such conflict-related issues as:

1. *Self-dealing (Section 4941).* The self-dealing rules essentially prohibit all transactions between a foundation and "disqualified persons" and their families. The act defines disqualified persons as substantial contributors to the foundation, the foundation's managers and trustees, and persons holding more than a 20 percent interest in a business or enterprise that has been a substantial contributor to the foundation. (The act also provides for exceptions. For example, a foundation may pay a disqualified person reasonable compensation for personal services to the foundation necessary to accomplish exempt purposes and, if certain requirements are met, may enter into certain limited dealings with disqualified persons.)

2. *Required distributions (Section 4942).* Since failure to expend funds had been cited as frequently associated with abuses, this provision is designed to prevent an unreasonable accumulation of foundation assets. The act requires a foundation to pay out in "qualifying distributions" the larger of its "adjusted net income" or the "minimum investment return" on the fair market value of the foundation's assets. The Tax Reform Act of 1976 permanently put the minimum investment return and thus the minimum required payout at 5 percent of a foundation's assets.

3. *Excess business holdings (Section 4943).* This series of rules is designed to reduce foundation holdings in and control of outside businesses. The Patman evidence showed conclusively that foundation control of businesses was the leading source of abuse. To avoid imposing excessive burdens on foundations with large holdings, the act distinguishes between holdings received by a foundation before and after May 26, 1969. For post-May 26, 1969, holdings, a foundation and related disqualified persons together may not own more than 20 percent (35 percent if a third person has effective control of the company) of the voting stock of a corporation. A foundation has five years after receipt of a holding to reduce it to the required level. For pre-May 26, 1969, holdings, the act provides for two phases of divestiture to bring a holding down to the 20 (or 35) percent level. In the first phase, which lasts ten to twenty years, depending on the original percentage, with longer periods for higher percentages, aggregate holdings of the foundation and disqualified persons must be reduced to 50 percent. In the second phase, which lasts fifteen years, the holdings must be reduced to 25 percent if disqualified persons own more than 2 percent, or 35 percent if they own less than 2 percent.

4. *Jeopardy investments (Section 4944).* A foundation may not make investments that would financially "jeopardize" the foundation's ability

to carry out its exempt purposes. (This provision does not apply to stock received from donors or investments made prior to 1970.)

5. *Disclosure (Section 6056).* All foundations with more than $5,000 in assets must file with the IRS such information as the names and addresses of foundation managers and substantial contributors; income, expenses, and disbursements; a balance sheet including detailed information about securities holdings; and the names of foundation managers with a 10 percent or greater interest in an outside business in which the foundation owns a 10 percent or greater interest. This information is available to the public.

Discussions with foundation executives, investment managers, state attorneys general, and others suggest that the prevalence of abuses, particularly at the major foundations, has been significantly reduced by the 1969 act. Law enforcement authorities, who, prior to the act, had taken an almost laissez-faire stance toward foundations, have since 1969 sharply increased the intensity of their oversight. Using the proceeds of a 4 percent tax on foundation investment income imposed by the 1969 act, the IRS has substantially added to the resources devoted to foundation audits. State attorneys general, who have broad powers over foundations because most foundations are organized under state law, have stepped up their surveillance. The effect of this swelling enforcement effort has been to drive out of business many small foundations established mainly to serve the donor's interest and to force larger foundations to abandon questionable practices for fear of penalties.

Many large foundations with large holdings of donor stock, such as the Robert Wood Johnson Foundation (Johnson & Johnson), the Edna McConnell Clark Foundation (Avon Products), and the Kresge Foundation (S. S. Kresge), have been selling off large portions of these holdings. The Mellon foundations have been reducing their massive positions in such Mellon-affiliated concerns as Gulf Oil Corp. and Aluminum Co. of America. Perhaps the most spectacular divestiture, though, is being conducted by the James Irvine Foundation, whose allegedly unscrupulous dealings with the Irvine Co., a large California landholder and developer of which the foundation owns 54.5 percent, were the subject of a report by Wright Patman. Because the 1969 act requires the foundation to reduce its holdings to 2 percent by 1979,* the company has

*The foundation must make this drastic reduction because Joan Irvine Smith, who is a disqualified person under the terms of the act, holds 22 percent of the company's stock.

decided to put itself up for sale. Offers from bidders including Mobil Corp. recently have ranged as high as $307.1 million.

In many cases, the ties between donors, their companies, and their foundations are becoming unraveled. Symbolic of this trend was the resignation of Henry Ford II as trustee of the Ford Foundation in early 1977. In his resignation letter to the foundation, Henry Ford was quite critical of the foundation's policies and staff and suggested the foundation was insufficiently appreciative of the capitalistic system that had made the foundation possible. Over the past twenty years, the Ford Foundation has followed a policy of continually divesting its giant position in Ford stock, which once comprised 88 percent of the total outstanding. The foundation now owns no Ford stock and has no members of the Ford family or executives of the Ford Motor Co. on its board of trustees. Its only tie to the family that founded it is its name.

The John A. Hartford Foundation also has changed, for more obviously compelling reasons. John A. Hartford's father was George Huntington Hartford, who, in the nineteenth century, had founded the Great Atlantic & Pacific Tea Co. John A. Hartford established the foundation in 1929, explicitly intending thereby to ensure continuity of control of the company "as we know it today."[4] For years, the trustees of the foundation loyally adhered to Hartford's intent. The foundation remained dominated by the company; Ralph W. Burger headed both the company and the foundation for twelve years. The foundation, which owned 34 percent of A&P's stock, steadfastly refused to cooperate with outsiders who considered taking over the company. Under foundation protection, the company's management became increasingly ingrown and the company stagnated.

By 1972, A&P's troubles had become acute. A desperation price-cutting campaign to revive sagging sales had produced staggering losses; in 1972, A&P lost $107 million.[5] The Hartford Foundation, which had about three-quarters of its assets in A&P, felt the full force of the company's traumas. As the price of A&P stock dropped from 70 in 1961 to 16 in 1972, the value of the foundation's A&P holdings shrank from $585 million to $135 million. The foundation became an object lesson, as one senior executive with another foundation puts it, on "what failure to diversify can cost charity." Meanwhile, A&P, which had been steadily reducing its dividend, eliminated it entirely, wiping out most of the foundation's income.

"It was very hard for them [the foundation trustees] to believe that A&P could really be in trouble," says Michael McIntosh, president of the Josephine H. McIntosh Foundation. (The McIntosh Foundation had most of its assets in A&P shares, which McIntosh, whose wife is an

A&P heir, had been unable to unload.) "Gradually," McIntosh recalls, "there was an awareness on the part of a sufficient number of the trustees of the foundation, probably helped out by the example of Penn Central, that even the finest companies if poorly enough managed for a long enough time can go down the tubes." In 1974, spurred by numerous disenchanted shareholders and the company's own board of directors, which had begun to worry mightily about shareholder suits, the Hartford Foundation took the lead in displacing the old management and bringing in a new chief executive from the outside. After massive retrenching and writeoffs, the new man appears to be in the process of turning A&P around. The foundation, meanwhile, has embarked on a diversification program. In June 1976, it sold through a public offering a fifth, or $21 million worth, of its once inviolate A&P holdings, reducing its percentage of the company's stock to 25.5 percent.

Today, few of the nation's large foundations show evidence of the egregious abuses and self-dealing of the sort highlighted in the 1960s by Wright Patman. But the conflicts of interest that remain, although often extremely subtle and perfectly legal, still permit foundations to serve as mechanisms for the perpetuation of corporate power and impair their ability to fulfill their responsibilities to help meet the nation's charitable needs. Few foundations conform to the standards set by the Ford Foundation—with its broad group of trustees, its diversified, professionally managed portfolio, its generous grant program (critics even argue that this generosity is severely depleting the foundation's assets), and its exclusive dedication to the public's well-being.

Two chief problem areas remain only marginally affected by the 1969 act:

1. Numerous foundations continue to possess extremely close links with donors, the donors' families, and the donors' companies. Although they have in some cases sold blocks of the donors' stocks, they have done so solely to comply with the 1969 act, and they clearly intend to continue holding as much stock as the law allows. The 1969 act limits the percentage of a company's stock a foundation can own, but it places no limits on the percentage of a foundation's portfolio that can be invested in a single stock; hence, many foundations continue to keep almost all their assets in shares of their respective donors' companies.

In many cases, substantial overlaps remain between a foundation's trustees, the donor and his family, and the associated company's management and board of directors. Trustees of such foundations typically continue to view the foundation as a mechanism for corporate control.

In conflicts between the charitable obligations of the foundation and the private concerns of the company, charity is likely to come off second best. Citing some of these relationships, Waldemar Nielsen, a prominent foundation critic, concluded that "the boards of the big American foundations are currently ridden with conflicts of interest incompatible with their objective and exclusive devotion to philanthropic purposes and the public interest."[6]

2. Despite the self-dealing rules, many foundations maintain very close ties with local banks and other organizations that provide them with services. In numerous cases, executives and directors of the bank serve as trustees, the bank serves as investment manager and custodian, and the foundation has invested heavily in the bank's securities and those of other companies represented on the board of trustees. As in the case of endowment funds, the relationships lessen the foundation's ability to secure disinterested, low-cost services and to employ its assets in the most productive way.

Because a large portion of their assets consists of tax money foregone by federal, state, and local governments, private foundations are really quasi-public institutions. Arguably (it is not the function of this report to make a judgment on the point), foundations serve an important social role and are entitled to their indirect public subsidy. But they are not justified in sacrificing their ostensibly charitable goals to serve the private interests of those who control them.

VII/The Donors and Their Companies

In 1945, Otto Haas, a German immigrant and founder of the Philadelphia-based Rohm and Haas Co., established a foundation and named it after his wife, Phoebe Waterman. In 1970, a year after her death and a decade after his, the foundation was renamed the Haas Community Fund. In 1975, its name was changed again, to the William Penn Foundation. Yet despite the increasingly cosmopolitan orientation implied by its name changes, and without violating the Tax Reform Act of 1969, the foundation remains as much a creature of the Haas family and of their company as it was in 1945.*

John C. Haas, Otto Haas's younger son, is chairman and president of the foundation and chairman of the company. F. Otto Haas, Otto Haas's elder son, is vice-chairman of the foundation and vice-chairman of the company. Also on the foundation's board of directors are the two Haases' wives and one of their sons. As of the end of 1975, all but $7,537 of the $124,048,622 in assets in the foundation's principal account was in 2,376,266 shares—18.5 percent of the total outstanding—of Rohm and

*Most of the information that follows on foundation holdings, trustees, and corporate relationships derives from the latest available foundation annual reports, foundation income tax returns (both 990-AR and 990-PF), corporation annual reports and proxy statements, and interviews by the author with foundation executives. The author is also greatly indebted to *The Big Foundations* by Waldemar Nielsen (a Twentieth Century Fund Study published by Columbia University Press), for background information on most of the major foundations.

Haas stock. These shares, combined with other shares controlled by the Haas family, make up 47.7 percent of the total.

The William Penn Foundation's holdings of Rohm and Haas do not violate the excess business holdings provision of the Tax Reform Act of 1969. But Rohm and Haas is not a big income producer for its shareholders. Recently, the stock was yielding about 2.8 percent in dividends. The foundation also receives income from several Haas family trusts. But in order to meet the minimum payout requirement, the foundation has had to sell small portions of its Rohm and Haas holdings.

Rohm and Haas has not been much of a capital gains producer for shareholders either. The stock was recently selling at its lowest price in seven years, down two-thirds from its 1973 high. The foundation's treasurer is unwilling to talk publicly about investment policy or any other aspect of his work, but the foundation has shown no sign of an intent to diversify its portfolio or to sell any more Rohm and Haas than necessary to meet the minimum payout requirement.

The nature of the charitable grants made by the William Penn Foundation has given it a reputation as one of the more innovative foundations. The Haas brothers take an active interest in philanthropy. But it appears that the foundation serves a dual purpose. During hearings on the 1969 act, a spokesman for the foundation told the Senate Finance Committee that it had been created "to establish a major philanthropy and to enable the family to satisfy their desire for such philanthropy without jeopardizing their control of the family business. . . . The company is a prime target for raiders and is protected only by the fact that as much as 49 percent of the stock can be considered in friendly hands."[1]

Whatever its charitable purposes, the William Penn Foundation is clearly an instrument for the retention of corporate control. An asset-rich chemical concern with sales of over $1 billion and a net worth of over $550 million, Rohm and Haas has often been regarded covetously by acquisition-minded conglomerateurs. The foundation's policy of keeping its entire portfolio invested in a single company whose stock pays a low dividend and has had a lackluster growth record is not the product of disinterested investment analysis and an effort to make the maximum amount available for charity in accordance with a prudent level of risk. It is, rather, the method by which the Haas-controlled board of directors of the foundation seeks to perpetuate the entrenched corporate position of the Haas family.

The 1969 Tax Reform Act penalizes investments that jeopardize a foundation's tax-exempt purposes. An instruction booklet issued by the IRS to assist foundations in complying with the act defines jeopardizing investments as "those which show a lack of reasonable business care and prudence in providing for the long- and short-term financial needs of the foundation."[2] The booklet further states: "to avoid the application of the tax on jeopardizing investments, a careful analysis of potential investments must be made and good business judgement must be exercised." (The booklet also notes that the IRS will not use hindsight in evaluating foundation portfolios for this purpose.) Because it was acquired before 1970, the William Penn Foundation's Rohm and Haas holding is exempt from these provisions. But it is hard to avoid the conclusion that the foundation's steadfast retention of Rohm and Haas stock has little to do with the exercise of reasonable business care and prudence or with the furtherance of the foundation's charitable purposes.

As the American economic system matures, the prevalence of large, family-run and -controlled corporations is declining, and although relatively common in the past, absolute family control of a company and its associated foundation is also becoming rare. Yet many large foundations still invest most of their assets in a single stock. Of the ten largest foundations, accounting for close to a third of all foundation assets, six, with assets of over $4 billion, have more than half their money invested in one company. Despite the limitations and intent of the 1969 act, all six of these foundations are the companies' largest single stockholders, and their blocks are essential for control of the company. Most one-stock foundations are dominated by a combination of relatives or descendants of the original donor and current or former executives of the donor's company. Over time, the descendants of donors have become dispersed and have tended to lose interest in the company or the foundation. Under these conditions, one-stock foundations increasingly are becoming simply adjuncts of the corporations—nonprofit, management-controlled holding companies. For the corporation executives in charge, the foundations are a valuable mechanism for resisting challenges and preserving their tenure in office.

Some examples of current foundation structure and control:

The Duke Endowment. Established by James B. Duke, founder of the Duke Power Co. (an electric utility serving North and South Carolina), this foundation, as of the end of 1975, had 75.3 percent of its $379,137,219 portfolio invested in Duke Power securities. Its common stock holdings represented 24 percent of the company's total shares outstanding. Of the fourteen trustees, two are family members (including James Duke's daughter), two are former executives or directors of Duke Power, one is a current director of the company, and three are executives with the foundation.

James Duke's trust indenture specified that the foundation's holdings were not to be changed "except in response to the most urgent and extraordinary necessity" and that if some securities were sold, the proceeds could be invested only in Duke Power securities or U.S. Treasury issues. In 1963, the foundation's trustees sought a South Carolina court judgment that would permit the foundation to diversify. But the request was turned down. Three years ago, they tried again and this time succeeded. But their purpose in seeking the court judgment apparently was not to sell Duke Power. Since the favorable decision, the foundation has disposed of most of the large blocks of Alcoa and Alcan Aluminum that also were among the original securities donated to the foundation by James Duke. John F. Day, secretary of the foundation, explains: "We think we lost the first case because we didn't convince the court we weren't talking about selling the Duke Power but some of the other things that we held." The foundation apparently made the point more clearly to the state court the second time. Beyond what may be necessary to comply with the 1969 act, the foundation does not contemplate reducing its Duke Power holdings.

In 1968, an official with the smaller, family-controlled Mary Duke Biddle Foundation, which also holds most of its assets in Duke Power stock and whose chairman is a trustee of the Duke Endowment, stated that its Duke Power holdings were "sacred." That attitude apparently continues to prevail among the family and corporate trustees of the Duke Endowment today.

The Lilly Endowment. As of the end of 1975, the Lilly Endowment had $687,730,590, or 90.3 percent of its assets, invested in Eli Lilly and Co. Its holding of 13,289,480 shares constitutes 19.25 percent of the company's outstanding shares. The foundation's eight-member board of directors includes: a member of the Lilly family, which started the foundation and the company; the present chairman of the company, the head of its finance committee, and two of its former presidents. (Eli Lilly, an early organizer of the company and honorary chairman of the board of trustees of the foundation, died in early 1977.) Another trustee is the chancellor of Indiana University, a major recipient of the foundation's grants. Five of the trustees are members of the board of Eli Lilly and Co. and are themselves major holders of Lilly stock. The foundation and the Lilly family together control 40.5 percent of the company. The foundation has sold off some of its Lilly shares to comply with the 1969 act but does not appear to be planning any further sales.

W. K. Kellogg Foundation. In conjunction with the Kellogg Family Trust, which it controls, this foundation held 36,176,480 shares of Kellogg Co., worth $917,978,180, as of August 31, 1976. This block, 95.1 percent of the foundation's assets, represented 49.1 percent of the company's outstanding shares. Of the foundation's nine directors, five are executives and/or board members of the Kellogg Co. (four of them own Kellogg stock), and they comprise the foundation's finance committee. Through sales of Kellogg stock, the foundation has complied with the 1969 act stipulation that it own under 50 percent of the company by 1979. The act also stipulates that the foundation should hold no more than 35 percent of the company by 1994. But according to foundation president Russell G. Mawby, the Kellogg Foundation has no immediate plans for further sales. As he puts it, "1994 is a long time away."

Many other one-stock foundations control important blocks of a company's securities and have links with the company.* For example, the Henry Luce Foundation (assets: $55 million) is dominated by current and former Time Inc. executives, their relatives, and members of the Luce family. The foundation has some 91 percent of its assets in Time Inc. stock. That block, plus blocks owned by two other foundations of which Time Inc. board members are trustees, makes up 9 percent of Time Inc.'s shares.

The Danforth Foundation ($106 million) has 84 percent of its money in Ralston Purina Co., a 5 percent ownership. William H. Danforth, chairman of the foundation's board of trustees, is a board member of the company, and Donald Danforth, Jr., another trustee, heads a Ralston Purina subsidiary.

Over half the assets of the Pew Memorial Trust ($485 million) and 95 percent of the assets of the J. Howard Pew Freedom Trust ($58 million) are invested in the Sun Co., accounting for close to 20 percent of total outstanding Sun Co. stock. The sole trustee for the foundations is the Glenmede Trust Co., which is controlled by the Pew family, which founded Sun Co. Among Glenmede's directors are the corporate secretary and a retired chairman of the Sun Co.

Virtually all of the assets of the Frank E. Gannett Newspaper Foundation ($150 million) are invested in shares of the Gannett Co. Those shares, as a result of the 1969 act, have been reduced through sales and donations from 27 percent to just under 20 percent of the total outstanding. Gannett Co. chairman Paul Miller is president and trustee of the foundation. Gannett Co. president Allen H. Neuharth and four other present or former Gannett officers and directors are trustees and officers

---

*The Twentieth Century Fund has 14 percent of its $28 million portfolio in shares of Federated Department Stores, Inc., which were donated to the foundation by Edward A. Filene, who established the foundation. None of the foundation's officers or directors is a director or officer of Federated.

of the foundation. All are Gannett stockholders; together, they own $10 million worth of the company's stock.

Similarly close foundation-corporation linkages are evident at the $34 million Rowland Foundation (Polaroid Corp.), the $45 million Boettcher Foundation (Ideal Basic Industries, Inc.), the $94 million Henry J. Kaiser Foundation (Kaiser Industries Corp.), and the $110 million Moody Foundation (American National Financial Corp.).

Other large nonprofit institutions closely allied with corporations escape the restrictions of the 1969 Tax Reform Act through a loophole that excludes "medical research organization[s] directly engaged in the continuous active conduct of medical research in conjunction with a hospital." The best-known organization that has attempted to take advantage of this loophole is the Howard Hughes Medical Institute (HHMI), a research facility in Miami, Florida, that was one of Wright Patman's prime targets. The HHMI was organized in 1963, when Howard Hughes transferred to it the shares of what was later called Hughes Aircraft Co., a major defense contractor. Hughes, who derived considerable tax benefits from the transfer,[3] installed himself as sole trustee, with complete control over HHMI's affairs. Hughes requested tax exemption for HHMI, but the IRS turned him down, maintaining that the institute was simply a tax dodge. In 1967, the IRS reversed itself, allegedly as a result of the efforts of Richard Nixon in return for a $205,000 Hughes Aircraft loan for his brother. In 1970, the HHMI applied to the IRS for a ruling that it is a medical research facility not covered by the 1969 act.

The IRS, as far as is publicly known, has yet to respond to this request. But whatever ruling emerges may have substantial financial consequences. As of this writing, the disposition of the Howard Hughes estate remains unsettled, and controversy continues to rage over which, if any, of several candidates was Hughes's legal will. During his lifetime, Hughes occasionally expressed the desire to make the institute his sole beneficiary, a move that would avoid taxes on the estate. The institute thus stands at least a good chance of eventually acquiring his estate, principally Summa Corp., a holding company for most of Hughes's other business properties. Shortly before he died, Hughes is said to have appointed as directors of HHMI Frank W. Gay, now president of Summa, and Chester C. Davis, Summa's chief counsel. Under the bylaws of the HHMI, the directors are to succeed Hughes as the institute's trustees.[4] If the HHMI obtains Summa, Summa's principal officers would then possess direct control, through a nonprofit institution, of corporate properties worth perhaps as much as $3 billion: $1 billion for Hughes Aircraft and $2 billion for Summa.[5]

If the IRS rules that the HHMI is a private foundation covered by the

1969 act, the institute will then have to divest controlling shares of Summa and Hughes Aircraft and substantially step up its contributions to charity. Hughes Aircraft has paid no dividends to the HHMI, which subsists instead on "distributions" from the company. These distributions amount to only $3.5 million, 0.35 percent of Hughes Aircraft's value. (In 1976, Hughes Aircraft earned about $60 million on sales of $116 billion.)[6] If the IRS rules that the HHMI is not covered by the 1969 act, the institute may become, in effect, a $3 billion, tax-exempt industrial complex controlled by Gay and Davis and not required to demonstrate more than minimal concern for charity.

A large foundation that has succeeded in taking advantage of the loophole is the Nemours Foundation. This institution is the beneficiary of and receives most of its income from the estate of Alfred I. Du Pont, one of the organizers of E. I. Du Pont De Nemours & Co. After he died in 1935, his estate was taken over by the Florida National Bank of Jacksonville and three individual trustees, the senior being Edward Ball, Alfred's brother-in-law. Ball built Du Pont's legacy into an immensely remunerative empire worth over $1 billion.[7] The estate holds large blocks of Du Pont and General Motors stock. But its principal asset is a 74 percent interest in the Jacksonville, Florida, based St. Joe Paper Co., which Ball built from a tiny paper mill into a sprawling conglomerate that, besides its extensive paper operations, controls two railroads, a sugar refinery, and "what is believed to be the largest and richest collection of real estate in Florida,"[8] including dozens of acres of downtown Miami.

Until 1970, most of the proceeds of this empire, usually between $10 million and $15 million a year and mostly from dividends from the Du Pont and General Motors stock, went to Alfred Du Pont's third wife, who was Ball's sister. In 1971, she died, and the money began flowing into the Nemours Foundation. The chief function of this foundation has been operation of the Alfred I. Du Pont Institute, a small hospital and research center for crippled children in Wilmington, Delaware. When it began its operations, the foundation sagely obtained a ruling from the IRS designating it as a medical research organization exempt from the 1969 act. With no payout rules to govern its operation, the money was soon piling up faster than the foundation seemed able or willing to spend it.[9] Recently, the foundation decided to appropriate some of its surplus, now over $50 million, for an addition to the hospital, but it has actually spent little of the money as yet.

Last year, Alfred Du Pont Dent, Alfred Du Pont's grandson and the only blood descendant of Du Pont on the Nemours Foundation board, commenced a series of moves to, among other things, broaden the foundation's activities and increase its return from the estate. His grandfather, Dent pointed out, had expressed the belief that "it is the duty of everyone in the world to do what is within his power to alleviate human suffering. . . ." His grandfather's will specified that the foundation should serve not only crippled children but also the elderly and "other worthy charitable institutions." Yet over the forty years in which he has managed Alfred Du Pont's estate, Ball appears to have been "dedicated more to the accumulation of economic power than the care of the needy."[10]

Dent's chief aim is to get the foundation to sell its interest in the St. Joe Paper Co., which in 1975 earned $187 a share but paid a dividend of only $4. The foundation has been reaping a return of just $280,000 on a 74 percent interest in an asset worth perhaps $500 million or more. If the foundation sold its St. Joe shares and invested the proceeds in more productive investments, Dent has claimed, it could increase its income and thus its distributions to charity by as much as $50 million annually.

Edward Ball and his associates vehemently oppose Dent's proposal. Along with three executives and directors of St. Joe and its subsidiaries, whom Ball, now eighty-nine and in failing health, wants to succeed him as stewards of the estate, Ball controls the foundation's six-man board of trustees.

Dent is not surprised by the opposition. "I think it is very difficult for people who work for the paper company to sit and vote whether they should sell the paper company," he says. If the Nemours Foundation were covered by the 1969 act, of course, it would already have had to prepare for divestiture of the paper company and been forced to increase its attention to charity substantially.

Meanwhile, the medical research loophole has attracted the attention of a number of estate planners, including those for John D. MacArthur, whose assets include virtually all of the stock in Bankers Life & Casualty, an insurance company worth perhaps $450 million, and enough Florida real estate to make him, if not a billionaire, very close to it.[11] MacArthur is eighty years old. His lawyers are reportedly exploring establishment of a medical research facility that could keep his assets untaxed and intact. How much money this arrangement would supply for charity—as opposed to further empire building—is unclear. During the years he has owned it, Bankers Life & Casualty has paid only a single dividend.

A trustee should act solely in the interest of the foundation and the furtherance of its charitable purposes. But if he is an officer, director, or stockholder of the allied company, or if he has an emotional or family tie to the donor of the foundation's stock, he may find it difficult to ignore the interests of the company, which may often be at variance with those of the foundation. Asked about the five individuals who are both officers or directors of Kellogg Co. and trustees of the Kellogg Foundation, foundation president Russell Mawby replies: "My experience is that the trustees act very responsibly and objectively and separate the two responsibilities very carefully. I see absolutely no conflict in their performance."

Yet, as in educational endowments, situations often arise in foundations that can subject the trustee with corporate affiliations to strains that he may feel compelled to resolve by favoring the company's management over the foundation's. Such situations include proxy fights and anti-management shareholder resolutions. It was recently reported, for instance, that a group of shareholders (including Frank Sinatra) was preparing a takeover fight against Del E. Webb Corp., an Arizona land developer and hotel/casino owner.[12] About 35 percent of the company's stock is held in the estate of Del E. Webb, who died in 1974. When Webb's estate is settled, the stock will go to the Del E. Webb Foundation. The executor of the estate and head of the foundation is Robert H. Johnson, the company's chief executive officer. According to *Business Week*, the company's "overall performance has been lackluster."[13] Yet it is difficult to believe that if a proxy fight developed, Johnson would decide it was in the best interests of the estate or the foundation to side with the insurgents.

The most flagrant example of trustees favoring their own interests over those of the foundation is, of course, the failure of one-stock foundations to diversify. It is no coincidence that at virtually every foundation that keeps most of its assets in the shares of a single company, the board of trustees is closely linked to the company. Willingness to permit such a concentration of assets runs directly counter to long-accepted standards of prudent investment management.* Among all the portfolios in the United States over which professional investment managers have discretion, it is difficult to find a single one that is more than 25 percent invested in a single company. In the $500 billion universe of professionally managed assets, the one-stock portfolios so common among private foundations are an anomaly. Everywhere else, prudence is synonymous with diversification.

Arguments against diversification, nonetheless, have been vigorously advanced by such foundations as Kellogg, whose shares have experienced substantial capital gains over the years. "We feel the general policy of holding Kellogg has served us well," says Russell Mawby.

*see p. 26.

"The performance of the stock has been dramatic and has far exceeded the general market indicators. If the idea of a foundation is to maximize the resources available for educational and charitable purposes, then society's interests would have been less well served if we had invested in something else." Executives of other foundations that have invested heavily in a single growth leader, such as Johnson & Johnson and S. S. Kresge, might make the same statement.

Most other one-stock foundations, though, have had their portfolios committed to less successful issues. For many years, the Grant Foundation, founded in 1936 by William T. Grant, was almost entirely invested in 1,294,000 common shares and 11,900 convertible preferred shares of W. T. Grant Co., the retail chain. In 1969, long before the company's troubles had become apparent, the foundation fortunately, at the urging of the New York State attorney general's office, began an active diversification policy and by the time the company went bankrupt in 1975, had reduced its holdings to 400,000 shares and accumulated a diversified portfolio now worth nearly $50 million. The remaining 400,000 shares, worth $20 million at the end of 1969, are now carried on the foundation's books for a nominal value of $1.

Other one-stock foundations invested in non-growth issues, such as the John A. Hartford Foundation, have made much less timely diversifications. Still others, such as the William Penn Foundation, have made negligible efforts at diversification despite the depreciation of their assets. The market value of the shares of Polaroid that company chairman Edwin Land and his family contributed to the Rowland Foundation, $94.2 million at the time of the gifts, was $33 million at the end of 1975. The Henry Luce Foundation's block of Time Inc. stock, most of which it received when Henry R. Luce died in 1967, at a cost basis of $68 million, was valued at $50 million at the end of 1975. The Moody Foundation's block of American National Financial Corp., valued at $103 million when the foundation received it, is now valued at only $85 million. Duke Power shares have been continuously falling for the last decade; now they are selling for half the price that prevailed in the 1960s.

One-stock portfolios, moreover, are much more volatile than well-diversified ones. Between the end of 1974 and the end of 1975, when the market as a whole was up, the market value of the Lilly Endowment's holding of Eli Lilly and Co. dropped $216 million to $688 million. To meet payout obligations, holders of a diversified fund can either use dividends and interest income or dispose of the least attractive issues in their portfolios. But one-stock foundations, particularly if the stock has a low dividend, often must sell portions of their principal holding. The

Lilly Endowment, for example, might have had to sell Eli Lilly shares at a time, such as 1975, when their price was unusually depressed.

One-stock foundations, by definition, are committed to equities and thus the stock market. But during such periods as the early 1970s, which featured desultory stock performance and high interest rates, the best-performing portfolios were those balanced between equities, debt securities, and money market or near-cash instruments. One-stock foundations cannot adjust to such shifts in the market.

The illiquidity of one-stock portfolios can present additional difficulties. In most cases, these large holdings consist of stock that has not been registered for public sale with the SEC. Small amounts of such stock can be sold under SEC Rule 144, which generally permits sales over a six-month period of an amount equal to the lesser of 1 percent of the company's outstanding stock or the average weekly trading volume. Unregistered shares also can be disposed of through private placements or swaps with other institutions. But major disposals to the public usually require a registered secondary offering, which can be conducted only with the participation and approval of the company. When an unexpected crisis afflicts a company in which a foundation with a diversified portfolio has a position, the foundation usually can unload its shares quickly and limit its losses. If the foundation instead holds a very large unregistered block, the company may refuse to cooperate in a secondary offering that could exacerbate its financial troubles and depress its stock. The foundation then has no choice but to watch its endowment shrink. Even when the company agrees to a secondary, the process of drawing up a prospectus, obtaining approval from the SEC, and organizing and conducting the sale can take months. Meanwhile, the company's shares may be falling drastically.

Explaining why the Kresge Foundation commenced a diversification program in 1965, when he became president, William H. Baldwin says, "As a trustee, I felt we had too many eggs in one basket. In a way, I'm sorry we didn't keep all the stock. If we'd held it, we'd be up to a billion and a quarter dollars instead of three quarters of a billion. But though we would have had an enormous corpus, it would have been absolutely illiquid and immobile." The foundation, which once had 95 percent of its assets in Kresge stock, has reduced its Kresge holding to a quarter of its portfolio. In part because of the stock's superior performance, S. S. Kresge Co. has been very cooperative with the foundation in arranging secondaries.

Because it may force a foundation to sell pieces of its major holding so that it can meet grant commitments and legal payout requirements, low yield is a particularly common and serious problem for one-stock foundations. In some cases, low yield may simply be a reflection of the company's lackluster earnings record. Shares of Sun Co. and Eli Lilly and Co. are selling for roughly the same price as a decade ago and pay out only 3 percent. This low yield has resulted in continual erosion in the holdings of the Pew Memorial Trust and the Lilly Endowment. A foundation exclusively invested in a stock with no growth, which pays a dividend below the 5 percent minimum payout, must inevitably run out of money.

In some cases, stocks have low yields because corporate managers prefer to use the company's income for other purposes. Unless they have reasons for behaving otherwise, corporate executives, spurred by, among other things, stock options and incentive bonuses, tend to be more interested in promoting capital growth than in paying generous dividends. They are inclined to increase dividends only when necessary to satisfy shareholders and attract buyers to their stock. The executives of a company that is largely or totally owned by a charitable foundation whose board of trustees is, in turn, controlled by the company are unlikely to feel pressure or to see reason to make large dividend payouts. As Julius Greenfield, then assistant attorney general of New York State, testified before Wright Patman's Subcommittee on Domestic Finance in 1973, "I don't think I have to tell this committee how easy it is for persons who administer foundations and who at the same time are interested in the closely held businesses themselves [owned by the foundations] to manipulate the closely held businesses so that there is little, if any, return to the foundation from those holdings of the foundation."[14]

In some instances, such niggardly payouts have come under attack, ironically, from members of the donor's family who still retain important shareholdings in the company, although they have lost control of the foundation to company executives. For example, the James Irvine Foundation owns 54.5 percent of the stock of the Irvine Co., whose executives dominate the foundation. For years, Joan Irvine Smith, who owns or controls 22 percent of the company's stock, has been waging a running battle with its management, which she accuses of deliberately and consistently understating the company's worth and earnings and paying out very stingy dividends.[15] Because nearly all the remaining stock is closely held by Irvine family members and the company's management, there is no public market for the stock; hence, its estimated value is usually derived from appraisals commissioned by the company and the foundation. By understating the value of its Irvine Co. holdings, of course, the foundation is able to reduce the amount of charitable benefits it is required to pay out under the 1969 act. In its annual report for the year ending March 31, 1976, the foundation valued its 4,590,000-

share holding of Irvine Co. stock at $94,095,000, or $20.50 a share. If this valuation was correct, the company was paying the foundation a dividend of 3.5 percent. (Before Joan Irvine Smith began her campaign, the company had been paying out much less.) But an investor group including Smith and Henry Ford II has offered $36 a share for the company,[16] which was recently topped by a bid from Mobil Oil for $36.50. If these offers fairly reflect the company's value, the foundation's actual yield from its Irvine Co. stock was less than 2 percent, and in that case, its charitable payments were over $3.5 million a year less than the minimum required by the 1969 act.

Noble Affiliates, Inc., is an Oklahoma oil concern organized by the Samuel Roberts Noble Foundation. As of April 1976, the foundation owned 70.5 percent of the company's stock. Sam Noble, chairman of Noble Affiliates, is a trustee of the foundation, as is E. E. Noble, his brother. Although in 1975 the company had retained earnings of $71.8 million, cash and marketable securities worth $4 million, and profits of $11.6 million, Noble Affiliates saw fit to pay out only $700,000 in dividends to the foundation. The foundation's yield on its holding was about 1.5 percent. Noble Affiliates' officers and directors, meanwhile, paid themselves direct and indirect remuneration of over $550,000. Sam Noble received $125,000. According to foundation president John March, "Their business needs a great deal of money for growth, and their growth is more important than increased dividends." However, in compliance with the 1969 act, the Noble Foundation will have to divest at least a portion of its stock in the company.

Many foundation executives argue that reinvesting earnings to promote growth instead of paying high dividends is in the best long-run interest of the foundation as well as the company. Such growth companies as Kellogg may have a modest current yield, but continuously rising earnings have permitted the company to increase its dividend to keep pace with the rising price of its stock. On the Kellogg Foundation's original investment, thus, the current yield is very high. According to this argument, mandated payout minimums frustrate foundations with growth stocks. If the payout is higher than the current dividend yield, the foundation will have to invade its corpus regularly and to sell shares that may later appreciate in value and might otherwise eventually make possible much higher payments to charity. Of course, very few foundations that follow the policy of earnings reinvestment have been as successful as Kellogg. Still, several one-stock foundations used these arguments effectively in lobbying for a reduction in the required payout provisions of the 1969 act.[17] In 1975, the payout level required under the 1969 act was 6 percent. In 1976, it was to have varied in accordance with prevailing money market rates and investment yields, with the annual adjustment limited to 0.25 percent. But due to foundation lobbying, the Tax Reform Act of 1976 set the payout permanently at 5 percent.

James Abernathy, a frequent critic of foundation policy, comments:

> It sounds like they're trying to do just what the 1969 act was trying to avoid, which is piling up money. Someone who donates stock to a foundation gets a tax advantage immediately. Other taxpayers have to make up for it immediately by paying higher taxes. But society doesn't receive any benefits from the foundation except over a long period of time, particularly if the dividend is low. What Congress wanted to do in passing the [1969] act was to make the return to society quicker.

Consider a hypothetical rich individual who gives $1 million worth of securities in his company to a foundation. If he is in the 70 percent tax bracket, the government immediately foregoes $700,000 in taxes as a result of his charitable contribution tax deduction. If he leaves the securities to a foundation upon his death, the government may lose an equivalent amount in estate taxes. If the stock given to the foundation yields 5 percent, it will just cover the foundation's current payout requirement. At that rate, charity will have to wait fourteen years to obtain $700,000 in benefits from the gift, not counting the interest the government could have earned (or might not have had to pay on its debt) during that time by collecting the money in taxes the first year.

If the gift of stock declined in value during those fourteen years, charity would have to wait even longer. For example, Edwin Land gave $94 million worth of Polaroid stock to the Rowland Foundation. His current salary at Polaroid is $235,280; so he may have taken a $66 million deduction. In addition, Land may have saved another $25 million by avoiding the capital gains taxes he would have had to pay if he had sold those shares.

Polaroid's price drop over the past few years has sharply reduced the value of the foundation's assets; hence, in 1975, the foundation paid out less than $1 million in grants. At that rate, charity will take a hundred years to reap the benefits of government's tax loss, again not counting interest. If the price of Polaroid's stock and thus the foundation's assets continue to fall, it could take even longer.

VIII/Banks and Brokers

"The very existence of a set of guidelines for the staff and board of a foundation serves to remind us from time to time of the possibility of conflict—or the appearance of conflict," says Irving Clark, a director of the Northwest Area Foundation in St. Paul, Minnesota. "Even though our intentions are good, it is helpful to be reminded."[1]

A couple of years ago, Clark drew up written conflict-of-interest guidelines for the foundation that, among other things, require foundation officers and trustees to disclose outside affiliations and to refrain from discussing and voting on matters in which they have a personal interest. Mostly as a result of the 1969 act, a number of other foundations, including Kellogg, Rockefeller, Ford, and Jerome, also have adopted formal conflict-of-interest rules. Other foundations, including Bush, Rosenberg, and Kresge, have informal policies. Lawrence Stifel, secretary of the Rockefeller Foundation, explains:

> The discussions leading to the Tax Reform Act revealed a degree of ignorance and suspicion of private foundations which has not been fully perceived by the foundation community. The political reaction against foundations emphasized the need for foundations to make every effort possible to maintain the highest fiduciary responsibilities of trustees and officers.

None of these guidelines has much effect on tight foundation-company-donor relationships; apparently, few trustees view these relationships as a conflict-of-interest problem. The guidelines focus on such conflict situations as the affiliation of trustees or foundation officers with organizations applying for grants and organizations that supply the

75

foundation with services.* But the effectiveness of the guidelines in dealing with these problems is questionable.

Despite the Northwest Area Foundation's policy, there is a clear conflict of interest on its own board of directors. Harry L. Holtz, director of the foundation, is chief executive officer and director of the First Trust Company of St. Paul. The chairman of the foundation's board is an advisory director of the bank. First Trust Company is the foundation's fiscal agent. It manages the portfolio and supplies the foundation with other banking services. The second largest holding in the foundation's portfolio is $4.3 million worth of stock in First Bank Systems, Inc., the bank holding company that owns First Trust Company. In other words, a trust company whose chairman is a trustee of a foundation manages the foundation's money and keeps the foundation heavily invested in the bank's own stock.

In its annual report, the Northwest Area Foundation discloses its relationship with the bank; this foundation is one of very few to disclose such information. The report also states that, in accordance with the foundation's written conflict-of-interest rules, the bank's chief executive officer "does not participate in or vote on board actions pertaining to the fiscal agent." In other words, at the meetings in which the directors of the Northwest Area Foundation discuss and vote on whether to renew First Trust Company's contract as fiscal agent, Harry L. Holtz remains in the room but dutifully keeps silent during the discussion and does not vote. Whether this permits the other directors to vote their minds freely is very questionable.

Conflicts involving advisors, brokers, and bankers, nevertheless, seem to be less common at foundations than at college and university endowments. One main reason, of course, is the self-dealing section of the Tax Reform Act of 1969. Another is that, because many foundation portfolios are relatively committed to a single stock, they usually are managed internally by the treasurer. And because foundations are under much less pressure for performance, even those with more diversified portfolios tend to be less actively managed than college or university endowment funds and thus generate fewer brokerage commissions. Many foundation portfolios, in fact, have changed little since they were received from the donors. Because of the relative paucity of their securities transactions and the relative simplicity of their cash management, the banking and custodial needs of foundations also are relatively simple.

*For example, in 1973 the Danforth Foundation made a $60 million matching grant to Washington University. William H. Danforth, chairman of the board of trustees of the foundation, is chancellor of the university.

Among foundations that produce sizable brokerage, however, the temptation to channel commissions to interested parties and to generate excessive commissions is always present. In 1973, Julius Greenfield of New York's attorney general's office told the Patman subcommittee that his office had encountered several cases of churning. In one instance, the foundation was under the control of a stockbroker who directed commissions to himself and unnecessarily traded the portfolio. Greenfield recovered the commissions and dissolved the foundation.[2]

Not all less-than-arm's-length brokerage arrangements involving foundations violate the prohibition against self-dealing. For example, the Boettcher Foundation in Denver discloses—in one of the rare "transactions with related party" footnotes in foundation annual reports—that "an officer of the Foundation is a partner of Boettcher and Co., an investment banking firm that buys and sell [sic] investments and performs certain other services, including securities valuations for the Foundation." That officer is E. Warren Willard, president of the foundation. Boettcher & Co., a New York Stock Exchange member firm, was founded by the same family that started the foundation. Willard, for many years the firm's managing partner, is still a limited partner and owns an interest in the firm.

Under the 1969 act, Willard is a disqualified person. But the self-dealing rules do not prohibit Willard or Boettcher & Co. from performing personal services for the foundation, including brokerage, if the services are reasonable and necessary to enable the foundation to carry out its tax-exempt purposes and if the compensation is not excessive. The footnote to the foundation's annual report states that the foundation's business dealings with Boettcher & Co. "are based on the prevailing rates and terms employed by Boettcher and Co. for similar customers."

But commission discounts offered by brokerage houses vary widely, and officials at the Boettcher Foundation, which manages its portfolio internally, may well feel some inhibition, given Willard's tie with Boettcher & Co. and his senior position at the foundation, in exploring the possibility of lower rates elsewhere.

Most of the conflicts of interest that affect services supplied to foundations seem to involve banks. Many foundations have strong links with banks that might inhibit the foundation from seeking the best banking services at the lowest cost. One of the most incestuous relationships, apparently, is that of the six foundations created by the Pew family with the Glenmede Trust Co.[3] Although very secretive, Glenmede Trust is known to be owned and controlled by the Pew family, which accounts for nearly all of its business. Among Glenmede's directors are several Pews, including R. Anderson Pew, secretary of the Sun Co., and several longtime Pew loyalists, such as Robert G. Dunlop, retired chairman and still a director of the Sun Co. Glenmede acts as sole trustee for all six of the Pew foundations and is also fiduciary or cofiduciary for several other family trusts and estates. In all, it has the power to vote 34.6 percent of the Sun Co.'s shares.

In establishing a fee level for Glenmede's services to the foundations, the Pew family is deciding, in effect, how much to pay itself. The foundation's tax returns suggest that the family's inclinations are toward generosity. In 1975, for instance, the Pew Memorial Trust, the largest of the six foundations, paid Glenmede $645,134 in fees. Precisely what Glenmede did for all that money is not known. But management of the foundation's portfolio cannot have consumed very much time. The portfolio consists of little more than shares of Sun Co. and a $222 million note from International Paper Co. received in return for the sale of shares in an oil company. (Glenmede received another $100,000 for computing the foundation's capital gain on the deal.) Unless Glenmede's fees can be proved to be excessive, the Pew family-Pew Memorial Trust-Glenmede relationship is in perfect compliance with the letter of federal law—even though the foundation is clearly a captive of the family that funded it and of the family's bank.

Other close associations between foundations and banks derive from the affiliation of the donor with the bank. For example, Karl Hoblitzelle, who created the Hoblitzelle Foundation in Dallas, was chairman of Republic National Bank of Dallas until shortly before his death eight years ago. Nearly all of his estate, including a sizable block of stock in the bank, went into the foundation. Today, the bank maintains a very close association with the foundation and with Karl Hoblitzelle's shares of Republic of Texas Corp., the holding company that owns Republic National. James W. Aston, chairman of Republic of Texas, is the president and a trustee of the foundation. Among the other trustees are James W. Keay, chairman of Republic National Bank, and two of Republic of Texas' other directors. All own stock in the bank. John M. Stemmons, a Dallas businessman on the bank's board, is the foundation's treasurer.

Republic National Bank manages the foundation's portfolio, the largest holding of which is Karl Hoblitzelle's old block, now $12.7 million worth of Republic of Texas Corp. Robert L. Harris, vice-president of the foundation, reports that the IRS conducted an audit of the foundation and that "they showed some interest" in the Republic of Texas holdings (which the bank is free to sell) as well as in the $4.8 million that was invested in eight other local banks. He adds: "They went into it very thoroughly but were satisfied." It is not known how much the foundation paid the bank for its services. The bank's published schedule reports that its investment management fee for portfolios the size of the Hoblitzelle Foundation is negotiable. In arriving at a fee for handling the foundation's business, the bank more or less negotiates with itself.

The George Gund Foundation was established by the former chairman of the Cleveland Trust Co. Prior to his death in 1966, George Gund also had been the bank's largest individual shareholder. The president of the foundation's board of trustees is Frederick K. Cox, executive vice-president of Cleveland Trust. George Gund's two sons are trustees of the foundation, directors of the bank, and owners of a total of $5 million worth of the bank's stock. Cleveland Trust is the foundation's custodian and the manager of its portfolio. In 1974, the bank was paid $44,657 for its services for the foundation. The portfolio's third largest holding is $1.9 million worth of CleveTrust Corp., the bank's holding company. Neither the George Gund Foundation nor the Hoblitzelle Foundation refers in its annual reports to its complex and close relationship with its bank.

The Mellon Bank, the largest in Pennsylvania, maintains similar relationships with the various Mellon-created foundations. The entire Mellon empire, in fact, is a dense thicket of corporate and family interconnections that often obscure the distinctions between business and charity. In recent years, several important family leaders have died, and according to some reports, the current generation of Mellons is unable or unwilling to fill the leadership vacuum. In the absence of such leadership, the Mellon family may not exert the concerted financial power that it once did.[4] But the Mellon fortune, estimated at between $3 billion and $5 billion, remains an immense financial force.

The three principal Mellon foundations are the Andrew W. Mellon Foundation ($610 million in investments), the Richard King Mellon Foundation ($225 million), and the Sarah Scaife Foundation ($71 million).

The Mellons who created the foundations were members of the second and third generations. Richard King Mellon, the family's financial leader until his death in 1970, was president of the Mellon Bank. (His great-grandfather founded it.) Seward Prosser Mellon is his adopted son. Sarah Scaife, who died in 1965, was his sister. Richard Mellon Scaife is her son. Paul Mellon is the son of Andrew W. Mellon, who died in 1937, and is Richard King Mellon's cousin.

The Mellon Bank is investment manager for the Andrew W. Mellon Foundation and the Sarah Scaife Foundation. The Mellon family owns about 40 percent of Mellon National Corp., the holding company for the bank.

Paul Mellon, trustee of the Andrew W. Mellon Foundation, owns 14 percent of Mellon National Corp. Although the foundation, like all of the Mellon foundations, has been diversifying from its Mellon-related industrial holdings, it still holds $225 million in Mellon-related companies, mainly Gulf Oil Corp. (Mellons are usually represented on the boards of companies, such as Gulf, in which they have major shareholdings.) It owns $20.2 million worth of Mellon National Corp.

Seward Prosser Mellon, trustee and chairman of the executive committee of the Richard King Mellon Foundation, is a director and a major stockholder of Mellon National Corp. The foundation has two-thirds of its assets in Mellon-affiliated companies, such as Gulf Oil, General Reinsurance Corp., and Alcoa. It also owns $16.3 million in Mellon Bank certificates of deposit.

Richard M. Scaife, chairman and trustee of the Sarah Scaife Foundation, is a director of Mellon National Corp. and owns 6 percent of its stock. The foundation owns $49.4 million in Mellon-related investments, including positions in Gulf Oil and First Boston Corp., an investment banking house that underwrites most Mellon-related issues, and $5.8 million in Mellon Bank certificates of deposit.

On a smaller scale, Elliott Averett, chairman of the Bank of New York, is a director of the Josiah Macy Jr. Foundation ($44.2 million in investments). The Bank of New York is the foundation's investment advisor.

Morgan Guaranty Trust Co. seems to be especially active in maintaining trustee and advisory/custodial relationships with foundation clients. They include the John and Mary R. Markle Foundation ($31.5 million in investments), of which Daniel P. Davison, senior vice-president of the bank, is a trustee, and the Alfred P. Sloan Foundation ($256 million in investments), of which Ellmore C. Patterson, chairman of the bank, is a trustee. The Alfred P. Sloan Foundation owns $4.7 million worth of stock in J. P. Morgan & Co. (the holding company for the bank) and the John and Mary R. Markle Foundation owns $1.2 million worth.*

Although these relationships are not necessarily sinister or excessively costly to the foundations involved, they do create conflicts of interest

---

*A number of banks hold very large—sometimes controlling—percentages of their own stock in trust department fiduciary accounts. For a large portion of those holdings, the banks have sole or partial voting power. The Cleveland Trust Co., for instance, holds 31.24 percent of CleveTrust Corp. stock in its trust department and has sole voting power over 11.93 percent. The Trust Company of Atlanta, Georgia, has 24.25 percent of Trust Company of Georgia stock in its trust department and has sole voting power over 12.61 percent.

for trustees who are bankers. And they may deter foundation officials from seeking out the best banking services at the lowest cost or from complaining about the banks' practice of putting shares of the banks' own stock in the foundation portfolio.

IX/Conclusions

Foundation critic Waldemar Nielsen has referred to "the almost limitless capacity of foundations to resist adaptation and self-improvement."[1] Apart from such exceptions as Ford, Carnegie, Hartford, and Kresge, which have moved decisively in the direction of becoming independent, nonconflicted institutions, most foundations today conform to Nielsen's description:

> The reforms which foundations most need all run directly against the grain of the thinking of most of the people who control them. From the perspective of the typical donor, diversifying the board and the portfolio and professionalizing the staff would mean depersonalizing his foundation, diluting his influence, and frustrating his dynastic ambitions. From the perspective of most trustees, such reforms would mean the ending of collegiality, the intrusion of unfamiliar people and alien ideas, the sharing of authority with nonbusiness professionals and intellectuals, and the commitment of the foundation to open dialogue and dispute. Their natural inclination has been, and presumably will be, to stand pat.[2]

Foundations also are afflicted by the same "golden goose syndrome" that impedes reforms at college and university endowments. Foundations cannot exist without the time and expertise provided by trustees and the money provided by donors. Cumbersome and annoying restrictions on trustees and donors may frustrate or eliminate their charitable inclinations. "I'm torn between having the field invulnerable to attack on the one hand yet making sure it can attract new money," says a senior foundation executive. "If you make the rules too tough, I'm concerned that you will lose a lot of money for charity."

A senior official at a large foundation also fears that strict rules governing trustee behavior would discourage the best qualified individuals from accepting foundation board memberships. "In choosing trustees," he says, "you face a trade-off between purity and ignorance. You want people who are informed and knowledgeable, who are experienced and in the prime of their working lives. But such people always have a lot of outside relationships. That's what makes them very valuable board members."

Granted, conflict situations are inescapable. The presence of businessmen on a board creates conflicts involving the selection of portfolios, banks, brokers, and investment managers. Educators, journalists, other foundation executives, and other intellectuals may have conflicts involving grants. The latter conflicts, though, may be more amenable than the former to control by such easily facilitated mechanisms as written guidelines. And even uncontrolled, they are less potentially detrimental to a foundation's long-term financial health.

Businessmen trustees may initially resist guidelines because they often view business arrangements with a foundation as a quid pro quo for their willingness to serve on the board. Yet business from the foundation seldom is very important to the trustee's company. Approached tactfully on the matter, such trustees may be willing to agree to a prohibition on these arrangements in the best interests of the foundation. In any case, most investment-related conflicts of interest involving foundations would be much less widespread if foundation boards included fewer businessmen and more individuals whose backgrounds qualify them to provide informed guidance on a foundation's charitable activities. Foundations, unlike educational endowments, do not depend on a continuing stream of gifts and therefore do not need to use board membership as a reward for important donor businessmen.

A number of foundation executives maintain that even existing controls on foundations imposed by the Tax Reform Act of 1969 have had a very repressive effect on foundations. They assert the act has reduced the birthrate of foundations and increased the death rate. However, the latest *Foundation Directory*, published by the Foundation Center, says: "We know the tax law tends to inhibit the birth of new foundations and encourages the dissolution of small ones, but thus far studies of birth and death rates have not revealed conclusive statistics for the whole field."[3] If, in fact, old foundations have been dissolved and new foundations have not been created, the 1969 act may indeed be responsible. The purpose of the act was to deter unscrupulous donors from using foundations as a mechanism for corporate self-dealing or other questionable purposes. If, as a result of the act, this practice has become less common, then fewer foundations may be better than more, from the public's perspective. If the donor's purpose is solely to serve charitable causes—while, of course, still enjoying a nice tax deduction—there is nothing in the 1969 act to deter him.

The trouble with the 1969 act is not that it is too harsh and repressive but that it does not go far enough. It does not really touch the abuses that result from the still tight interconnections between many foundations, donor families, and companies. Conflicts at educational endowments tend to diminish over time, as financial and other pressures force trustees to realize that the old ways of management by crony are not serving the best interests of the school. But foundations do not confront the same pressures as educational endowments and are free to continue to pursue self-interested goals. Foundations would be well-advised to take many of the same voluntary steps recommended for educational endowments, such as the adoption of disclosure procedures beyond those required by the 1969 act.* But without the stimulus of new legislation, foundations almost certainly will not initiate such measures.

In April 1973, at the opening of hearings by his Subcommittee on Domestic Finance, Wright Patman remarked:

> The recent happenings on Wall Street have shed light upon a major problem currently confronting the foundation community, that is, the fact that many foundations find themselves in a position where their entire portfolio is made up of the stock of one or two corporations. Thus, the foundation trustees and managers are placing the fate of their charitable beneficiaries in the hands of the managers and executives of these corporations.
>
> This excessive concentration of investment unquestionably increases the risk of loss and places in jeopardy the fate of the charitable beneficiaries. The portfolio of a private foundation is no place for such imprudent investment policy.
>
> There is considerable evidence that private foundations which have failed to diversify their portfolios have deprived their charitable beneficiaries of many millions of dollars.
>
> Another major criticism of private foundations is that their governing boards fail to reflect in membership and philosophy the constituency they are intended to serve. The incestuous interlocking of the directors and trustees of private foundations with the family of the donor or with the officers and directors

*See pp. 56-57.

of the donor or foundation controlled corporation has served to perpetuate a group that in no way reflects the charitable beneficiaries it must serve.

If, in a sense, foundations are a "public trust," then the needs of the public must be placed above those of the alma mater.[4]

Patman had called these hearings to discuss two new pieces of reform legislation applicable to foundations. But the strong public sentiment for reform that had swept in the Tax Reform Act of 1969 was all but exhausted, and Patman's bills died, in part because of strong opposition from several major foundations. Today, the problems they were designed to solve are still with us. As a reasonable and nonstultifying approach to conflicts of interest at foundations, the proposed legislation deserves renewed consideration.

The bill that was labeled H.R. 5729 would have forced portfolio diversification by amending the definition of a jeopardizing charitable investment to include "nondiversified holdings." The bill defined a nondiversified holding as "the amount (if any) by which the value of a private foundation's holdings of stock and debt obligations of any corporation exceed 10 percent of the value of the total assets of the private foundation."[5] It would have given foundations five years after the bill became law to comply.

Such a law would substantially reduce—even destroy—the value of many essentially one-stock foundations to the businessmen who control them. Many of these businessmen might even resign from their trusteeships, creating opportunities for the recruitment of more philanthropically minded individuals to foundation boards. Foundations might then be able to increase their concentration on charity.

Patman's other bill, H.R. 5728, could also have far-ranging, if less dramatic, consequences. It would have funneled a major portion of the 4 percent excise tax collected from foundations by the IRS to state agencies, enabling them to increase their supervision of private foundations "to insure that such private foundations will promptly and properly use their funds for charitable purposes."[6] The IRS, whose regulatory efforts over foundations are regarded by many observers as lackluster and often ineffectual, is generally limited to taxation as an enforcement mechanism. State laws applicable to foundations are far broader and far more flexible, and officials of some states have been very aggressive in enforcing them. The state laws are usually based on the common law notion that, because it is virtually impossible for a particular individual to prove that he is the intended beneficiary of a foundation and thus has standing to take court action against the foundation, the state must serve as a representative of the public and enforce charitable dispositions for the public benefit. Many state laws give the attorney general the same standing as a director or officer of the foundation in effecting changes and make him a party to all court proceedings involving charitable distributions. In 1973, having performed such functions in his capacity as assistant attorney general for New York, Julius Greenfield told the Patman committee:

> The federal approach, the imposition of sanctions, certainly has a deterrent effect upon improper foundation administration. But it only goes part of the way. It does not provide, and there is some doubt that it can, for the various kinds of court and administrative actions that are available to the state attorney general. These would include imposition of personal responsibility on foundation managers for improper administration, removal of officers and directors and appointment or election of new officers and directors, dissolution of foundations and distribution of their assets to public charities and requiring a full judicial accounting of the activities of foundation administrators.[7]

Greenfield cited as an example of his office's enforcement a case where

> . . . a very detailed investigation and examination of the foundation directors revealed extensive areas of self-dealing, waste, and failure to make the assets productive. The major holding of the foundation consisted of control holdings in several business corporations, in which the foundation managers were principal officers and directors. As such they received very handsome compensation. As a result of our efforts the following occurred: (1) the board of directors of the foundation was increased to include disinterested directors who would constitute a majority on the board; (2) the foundation was to be represented on the board of directors of the business corporations by one of the new directors; (3) the foundation would and has adopted a plan of dissolution and distribution of its assets to charitable institutions; and (4) this distribution, which may approximate $14,000,000, will be made to eligible charitable beneficiaries within a year.[8]

In Minnesota, local officials, including the state attorney general, took the lead during the 1960s in totally overhauling and reforming the Bush Foundation, which was established by one of the leading figures in Minnesota Mining and Manufacturing and held nearly all of its assets in 3M stock.[9] The Bush family spent a number of years struggling with 3M executives for control of the foundation; during this period, both sides participated in a number of dubious transactions. Finally, the attorney general and a state court reorganized the foundation's board of directors to include a majority of independent trustees, none of whom is permitted to own more than a 5 percent interest in any profit-making corporation.

With the aid of Brown Brothers Harriman & Co. and United States Trust Co. in New York and The Northern Trust Co. in Chicago, the foundation divested the 3M shares and invested the proceeds in a diversified portfolio now worth $125 million.

Not all states enforce their laws pertaining to charitable institutions with such vigor. But with federal financial assistance and encouragement from a law modeled after H.R. 5728, many more might make the effort.

Reform of foundation conflicts of interest will not come easily. The notion that foundations are not a public trust but the personal property of the donor, his family, or his company remains widespread. When asked, at a business luncheon a few years ago, why his foundation had never issued an annual report or any other report to the public, J. Howard Pew shouted, "I'm not telling anybody anything. It's my money, isn't it?"[10] Not until the still extensive interlocks between donors, companies, and foundations are broken for good can the nation's private foundations rid themselves of still common but avoidable conflicts of interest and devote themselves exclusively to charity.

Footnotes

Author's Preface

1. *1976 Fact Book*, The New York Stock Exchange, p. 53.
2. SEC, *Statistical Bulletin*, May 1976, vol. 35, no.5.
3. Ibid.

Chapter I

1. *Ford Foundation Annual Report*, 1966, p. 7.
2. See *Managing Educational Endowments: Report to the Ford Foundation*, Advisory Committee on Endowment Management, 2nd ed., 1972.
3. For an analysis of the changes in endowment fund policies after the Bundy statement, see Chris Welles, "University Endowments: Revolution Comes to the Ivory Tower," *Institutional Investor*, September 1967, p. 11.
4. J. A. Livingston, "How Howard Butcher Handled Sales of Penn Central Stock," Philadelphia *Evening Bulletin*, December 9, 1970, p. 1.
5. The best sources of statistical data on the structure and policies of endowment fund management are: Louis Harris and Associates, Inc., *Managing Endowment Funds: A Survey of Endowed Institutions*, 1971, which surveyed 660 nonprofit institutions including 214 colleges and universities; and *Results of the 1975 NACUBO Comparative Performance Survey and Investment Questionnaire*, National Association of College and University Business Officers, 1975, which surveyed 157 pooled endowment funds. Additional data based on a survey of 383 colleges and universities are contained in William L. Cary and Craig B. Bright, *The Developing Law of Endowment Funds: "The Law and the Lore" Revisited* (New York: The Ford Foundation, 1974).
6. The situation is discussed in detail in James Ridgeway, *The Closed Corporation*

(New York: Random House, 1968). See also Richard J. Barber, *The American Corporation* (New York: E. P. Dutton & Co., 1970), pp. 99–107.

7. "Colleges Go into Business to Make Ends Meet," *U.S. News & World Report,* January 27, 1975, pp. 33–34.

8. Barber, *The American Corporation,* p. 105.

9. *Funds for the Future,* a background paper by J. Peter Williamson for the Twentieth Century Fund Task Force on College and University Endowment Policy, 1975, p. 74.

10. Harris, *Managing Endowment Funds,* p. 26.

11. Charles C. Abbott, *Trusteeship in Profit Corporations and Non-Profit Organizations* (Cambridge, Mass.: The Cheswick Center, 1974), p. 19.

12. *Stern et al. v. Lucy Webb Hayes National Training School for Deaconesses and Missionaries et al.,* 381 F. Supp. 1003 (D.C.D.C. 1974).

Chapter II

1. Charles Ellis, *Institutional Investing* (Homewood, Ill.: Dow Jones-Irwin, Inc., 1971), p. 188

2. Prefatory note to the Uniform Management of Institutional Funds Act drafted by the National Conference of Commissioners on Uniform State Laws, 1972, p. 4. Versions of this act have been passed by the legislatures of several states.

3. *Blankenship v. Boyle,* 329 F. Supp. 1089, 1096 (D.C.D.C. 1971).

4. Comment on Section 6 of the Uniform Management of Institutional Funds Act, p. 14.

Chapter III

1. *The President's Report, 1975–1976,* California Institute of Technology, November 1976, p. 123.

2. Statement of John G. Simon, Hearings on Private Foundations, Subcommittee on Foundations, U.S. Senate, October 2, 1973, p. 178.

3. *Restatement of Trusts (Second),* Sec. 228 (1957).

4. Employee Retirement Income Security Act of 1974, Sec. 404 (a) (1) (C).

5. Marion Fremont-Smith, *Foundations and Government* (New York: Russell Sage Foundation, 1965), p. 100.

Chapter IV

1. A sampling of some of the major articles: "On the Average: More Pension Funds Try to Tie the Market Instead of Beating It," *The Wall Street Journal,* November 12, 1975, p. 1; "Much Ado About Index Funds," *Institutional Investor,* February 1976, p. 17; "Tieing Your Investments to the Indexes," *Money,* May 1976, p. 87; "Index Funds —An Idea Whose Time Is Coming," *Fortune,* June 1976; "Queering Wall Street's 'Money Game,'" *The Nation,* March 12, 1977, pp. 300–304.

2. Three recent books accessible to the layman that describe efficient market theory: James H. Lorie and Mary T. Hamilton, *The Stock Market: Theories and Evidence* (Homewood, Ill.: Richard D. Irwin, 1973); Burton G. Malkiel, *A Random Walk Down*

Wall Street (New York: W. W. Norton, 1973); Richard A. Brealey, *An Introduction to Risk and Return from Common Stock* (Cambridge: The M.I.T. Press, 1969).

3. "Why Money Managers Like Index Funds," *Business Week*, December 20, 1976, p. 54.

4. For a lucid study that discusses the difficulties presented by the efficient market thesis for endowment funds, see Burton G. Malkiel and Paul B. Firstenberg, *Managing Risk in an Uncertain Era: An Analysis for Endowed Institutions* (Princeton: Princeton University Press, 1976).

5. *1975 NACUBO Comparative Performance Survey*, p. 5.

6. Edward S. Herman, *Conflicts of Interest: Commercial Bank Trust Departments*, Report of the Twentieth Century Fund Steering Committee on Conflicts of Interest in the Securities Markets (New York: The Twentieth Century Fund, 1975), pp. 89–105.

7. For a recent account of commission rate competition, see Chris Welles, "Discounting: Wall Street's Game of Nerves," *Institutional Investor*, November 1976, p. 27.

8. *Funds for the Future*, p. 165.

9. "A Fund to Prop Up Colleges," *Business Week*, January 20, 1975, p. 45.

Chapter V

1. *Stern et al. v. Lucy Webb Hayes National Training School for Deaconesses and Missionaries et al.*, 381 F. Supp. 1003 (D.C.D.C. 1974). The case grew out of a newspaper article: Ronald Kessler, "Trustees' Banks Use Hospital Money," *Washington Post*, February 4, 1973, p. 1.

2. Myles M. Mace, "Standards of Care for Trustees," *Harvard Business Review*, January-February 1976, p. 15.

3. *Stern et al. v. Lucy Webb Hayes National Training School for Deaconesses and Missionaries et al.*, p. 1015.

4. *Guidelines for Resolution of Conflicts of Interest in Health Care Institutions*, American Hospital Association, 1974.

5. *Stern et al. v. Lucy Webb Hayes National Training School for Deaconesses and Missionaries et al.*, p. 1019.

6. Mace, "Standards of Care for Trustees," p. 22.

7. *Stern et al. v. Lucy Webb Hayes National Training School for Deaconesses and Missionaries et al.*, 367 F. Supp. 536 (D.C.D.C. 1973).

8. Mace, "Standards of Care for Trustees," p. 28.

9. *Ibid.*, p. 148.

10. *Stern et al. v. Lucy Webb Hayes National Training School for Deaconesses and Missionaries et al.*, 381 F. Supp. 1003 (D.C.D.C. 1974), p. 1016.

11. William C. Porth, "Personal Liability of Trustees of Educational Institutions," *The Journal of College and University Law*, Vol. 1 (Fall 1973), p. 88.

12. *Giving in America: Toward a Stronger Voluntary Sector*, Report of the Commission on Private Philanthropy and Public Needs, 1975, p. 175.

13. *Industry Audit Guide: Audits of Colleges and Universities*, Committee on College and University Accounting and Auditing, American Institute of Certified Public Accountants, Inc., 1973, p. 9.

14. For an analysis of current practices, see *Funds for the Future*, pp. 135–142.

15. "Related Party Transactions," *Statement on Auditing Standards*, American Institute of Certified Public Accountants, Inc., July 1975, p. 2.

Chapter VI

1. *Congressional Directory*, August 7, 1961, p. 13755.

2. *The Foundation Directory*, Edition 5 (New York: The Foundation Center, 1975), pp. xii–xiv.

3. The Patman reports are entitled *Tax Exempt Foundations and Charitable Trusts: Their Impact on Our Economy*, Subcommittee Chairman's Report to Subcommittee No. 1, Select Committee on Small Business, House of Representatives. They are dated: December 31, 1962; October 16, 1963; March 20, 1964; December 21, 1966; April 28, 1967; March 26, 1968. Two additional reports were issued on June 30, 1969, and August 1972. In addition to these reports, useful accounts of the activities of foundations during this period are Waldemar A. Nielsen, *The Big Foundations*, A Twentieth Century Fund Study (New York: Columbia University Press, 1972); Joseph C. Goulden, *The Money Givers* (New York: Random House, 1971); Ferdinand Lundberg, *The Rich and the Super Rich* (New York: Lyle Stuart, 1968), pp. 465–530 (paperback); Ovid Demaris, *Dirty Business* (New York: Harper's Magazine Press, 1974), pp. 252–325; Ralph L. Nelson, *The Investment Policies of Foundations*, A Foundation Center Study (New York: Russell Sage Foundation, 1967).

4. Nielsen, *The Big Foundations*, p. 177.

5. For an account of this period, see Eleanor Johnson Tracy, "How A&P Got Creamed," *Fortune*, January 1973, p. 103.

6. Nielsen, *The Big Foundations*, p. 317.

Chapter VII

1. Quoted in Nielsen, *The Big Foundations*, p. 240.

2. *Tax Information for Private Foundations and Foundation Managers*, Internal Revenue Service, U. S. Department of the Treasury, September 1975, pp. 50–51.

3. See Demaris, *Dirty Business*, pp. 259–266.

4. Wallace Turner, "Petition Could Validate a 'Lost' 1938 Hughes Will," *The New York Times*, January 13, 1977, p. 20.

5. "The Secret World of Howard Hughes," *Newsweek*, April 19, 1976.

6. For information on the Howard Hughes Medical Institute submitted by the institute to Congress, see Hearings on Tax Exempt Foundations and Charitable Trusts, Subcommittee on Domestic Finance, U.S. House of Representatives, April 5–6, 1973, pp. 140–170.

7. See Rush Loving, Jr., "Ed Ball's Marvelous, Old-Style Money Machine," *Fortune*, December 1974, p. 170, and Phyllis Berman, "The Strange Case of Ed Ball," *Forbes*, February 15, 1977, pp. 63–66.

8. Loving, op. cit., p. 171.

9. See a series of articles on the foundation by Curtis Wilkie in the *Wilmington (Del.) Evening News*, March 19 and March 29, 1974, reprinted in Hearings on Private Foundations, Subcommittee on Foundations, U.S. Senate, May 13, 14, and June 3, 1974, pp. 140–146.

10. Robert D. Shaw, Jr., "Du Pont Trust: Where Will the Money Go?" *Miami Herald*, August 1, 1976, p. 1. See additional articles by Shaw in the *Miami Herald* on November 15 and 19, 1976.

11. See Lewis Berman, "The Last Billionaire," *Fortune*, November 1976, p. 132.

12. "Sinatra Wants More of the Webb Action," *Business Week*, April 11, 1977, pp. 30–31.

13. *Ibid.*, p. 30.

14. Hearings on Tax Exempt Foundations and Charitable Trusts, Subcommittee on Domestic Finance, p. 200.

15. For background on the Irvine Foundation, see Nielsen, *The Big Foundations*, pp. 126–134. For a recent statement on Joan Irvine Smith's allegations, see Hearings on Private Foundations, Subcommittee on Foundations, pp. 185–201. For a recent account of the Irvine Co., see Wyndham Robertson, "The Greening of the Irvine Co.," *Fortune*, December 1976, p. 84.

16. *Wall Street Journal*, March 3, 1977, p. 5.

17. Eileen Shanahan, "House Tax Panel Eases Rule on Foundation Spending," *The New York Times*, October 14, 1971, reprinted in Hearings on Tax Exempt Foundations and Charitable Trusts, Subcommittee on Domestic Finance, pp. 21–22.

Chapter VIII

1. Much of the information on conflict-of-interest guidelines that follows is derived from Frederick Williams, "Are Written Guidelines Useful?" *Foundation News*, May/June 1977, p. 51.

2. Hearings on Tax Exempt Foundations and Charitable Trusts, Subcommittee on Domestic Finance, p. 182.

3. For background on the family, see Michael C. Jensen, "The Pews of Philadelphia," *The New York Times*, October 10, 1971, Section 3, p. 1.

4. See Michael C. Jensen, "An Old Fortune Moves On," *The New York Times*, May 2, 1971, Section 3, p. 1.

Chapter IX

1. Nielsen, *The Big Foundations*, p. 431.

2. *Ibid.*, p. 443.

3. *The Foundation Directory*, pp. xiii–xiv.

4. Hearings on Tax Exempt Foundations and Charitable Trusts, Subcommittee on Domestic Finance, pp. 1–2.

5. *Ibid.*, p. 5.

6. *Ibid.*, p. 3.

7. *Ibid.*, p. 183.

8. *Ibid.*, p. 181.

9. Nielsen, *The Big Foundations*, pp. 121–123.

10. *Ibid.*, p. 126.